The Lure of Antique Arms

The Lure of

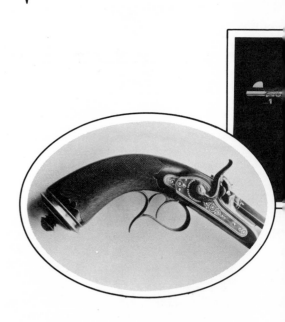

Merrill Lindsay

Antique Arms

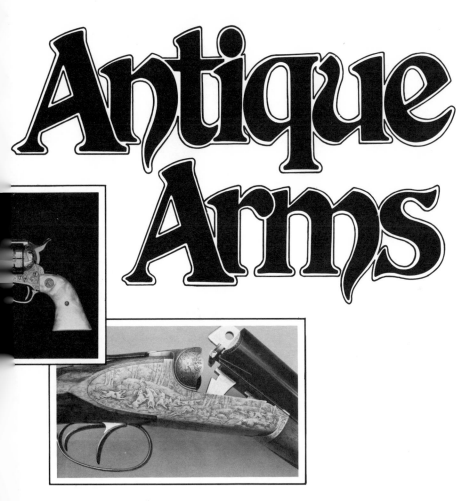

DAVID McKAY COMPANY, INC. New York

Library of Congress Cataloging in Publication Data

Lindsay, Merrill.
    The lure of antique arms.

    Bibliography: p.
    Includes index.
    1. Firearms—Collectors and collecting.
I. Title.
TS532.4.L56   739.7'4'075   74-25989
ISBN 0-679-20299-4

MANUFACTURED IN THE UNITED STATES OF AMERICA

Designed by Bob Antler

Preface

Weapons have always fascinated men. Today the older, more decorative or historic firearms are eagerly sought after by collectors, young and old, rich and not-so-rich. Some knowledge of firearms is necessary if the beginning collector is to enjoy what he collects and especially if he hopes to profit from his collecting.

The rewards of knowing what you are collecting can be enormous. I know. I collected the wrong guns for years. By wrong, I mean I got a kick out of what I collected, but at the end of those years the guns in my collection were barely worth what I paid for them. During the same time, the guns which belonged to smarter collectors than I rose in value four times what was paid for them. That was when I started to read and learn about what I was collecting. It has paid off many times.

In this book I will first give the beginning collector a guide to identifying the basic types of firearms. There are illustrations and descriptions which show the difference, for example, between a hand cannon and a flintlock. I have also listed different collections scattered around the United States where these arms can be seen and studied.

As recognition and identification of arms becomes easy, the collector will find he likes certain types of weapons better than others. Thank goodness for that. Otherwise there would not be enough single-action Colt Frontiers to go around. What an individual person wants to collect will depend on his own point of view.

Some collectors are mechanically inclined. They will be interested in the more ingenious mechanisms of the nineteenth and twentieth centuries. The inventions by Yankee gunsmiths of repeating and automatic weapons will appeal to the collector who will go after his newest acquisition with a screwdriver to see how it works. He will try to find out at what point and on what model a minor improvement makes one Smith & Wesson more valuable than another.

Another type of collector will become a history buff. He may have been a bum in history class when the teacher was trying to tell him why Washington crossed the Delaware, but once he owns a Kentucky rifle, or an American Committee of Safety musket, he will want to know as much as he can about the men who carried those guns—who, where, when, why and how they fought.

A third type of collector will be interested only in good design and beautiful workmanship: the way a gun is decorated; the lifelikeness of the hunting scenes engraved on the receiver; the nice balance of the weapon and the fine condition of a well cared for antique.

Whatever your interest in firearms, you will find good basic rules must be observed if you are to be a successful collector. Quality, rarity, age, are all factors. How you balance each will determine how your collection goes up in value. A smart collector will trade less valuable guns for better ones and stretch his dollar investment. Good collections, large and small, have gained in value at a much higher rate than stocks and bonds, real estate or practically any other investment you can think of. Collecting can be deeply satisfying—and lots of fun.

While some old guns can be found in antique shops, sporting goods stores and occasionally in attics, the bulk of the buying and selling of collector's items is done at gun shows. Every state has its own collectors club. In addition, there are city clubs, area clubs and regional clubs. Each has meetings and swap sessions. Two, three, or four times a year, the state clubs have public gun fairs where hundreds of collectors and dozens of dealers will have tables of guns and accessories for sale and swap. There are also big regional shows where thousands come from all parts of the country not only to buy, sell and swap but to exhibit fine weapons arranged in educational exhibits that compete for prizes.

Finally, there is a whole new breed of collector who collects commemorative arms. These new reproductions of historic arms are issued mostly by the major arms companies in limited editions. These are usually specially packaged or cased, with identifying plates that tell the history of the weapon and often show the number of the gun in its limited edition. While these new collector's items have only been issued during the past dozen years or so, some have gone up in value enormously; others have not. Again, you must know the tricks before you buy one commemorative instead of another.

For the next few years there will be a flood of Bicentennial weapons. They will be issued from now until the Bicentennial of the War of 1812. Then they will probably go right on till the Bicentennial of the Civil War. Here, a key question to ask is, How many of these reproductions of one historic weapon have been made? Other questions you will have to answer for yourself are, How well is the reproduction made? Is it made of the identical materials as the original? Is it a faithful reproduction? Is it in scale? Does it function? If the answer to these questions is "yes," and not too many of these reproductions are being made, your commemorative is a good buy, especially if it is an exact copy of a historic weapon. For example, if there is only one pair of silver mounted pistols that belonged to George Washington and it is in the West Point Museum, you know neither you nor any other person will ever own it. A reproduction of it, if well done, is a good investment.

I know a number of men who started their gun collections in their early teens. Today their collections are irreplaceable. This has happened for two reasons. One was their skill in collecting; the other I have mentioned: the tremendous increase in the value of antiques has made a gun they bought ten years ago so expensive that they couldn't afford to buy it today. One collector I know started a swap list which he copied on a home duplicating machine and mailed to friends and collectors. He kept on trading and upgrading his own collection all the way through school. When he graduated from college he surprised his father by offering to give him back all of the money that the father had spent to send him to school. Besides the money he had saved, he had the beginning of one of the ten best collections in the United States.

I could have called this introduction: "Collecting for Fun and Profit," but really, deep down, it's been the fun that has kept me going as a collector. I might have been richer if I had taken up accounting . . . if I could have learned to count really fast.

Contents

A Glossary of Arms Collectors' Terms

ARQUEBUS: antique gun smaller than a musket

AUTOMATIC: a gun that continues to shoot as long as you hold the trigger. Incorrectly used to designate an autoloader

BANDOLEER: cartridge belt slung over the shoulder

BARREL: every gun has a barrel through which the bullet passes

BATTERY (frizzen, steel): the piece of steel that sparks when hit by the flint.

BERSELLI: Florentine inventor of a repeating loose-powder-and-ball flintlock

BLACK POWDER: gunpowder made with charcoal, saltpeter and sulfur

BLUING: protective oxide on steel gun parts

BREECH LOADER: a gun loaded from the back of the barrel

BREECH PLUG: steel cap which closed the rear of a muzzle-loader barrel

BROWN BESS: the military musket used by the British between 1720 and 1840

BULLET: the projectile propelled by gunpowder

CALIBER: the bore or internal diameter of a gun barrel

CALIVER: arquebus, antique matchlock gun smaller than a musket

CARBINE: short-barreled rifled arm suitable for cavalry

CARTRIDGE: powder and ball and, later, powder, ball and primer in a package

CASE: fitted box for gun or pistols

CASE HARDENED: varicolored heat-treated steel surface

CHARGE: a measured amount of powder

COCK: hinged arm on a wheel lock or flintlock which holds pyrites or flint

COEHORN: a Baron Coehorn invented the foot (infantry) mortar

CRUD: the residual dirt from black powder combustion

DAG: old term for a heavy wheel-lock horse pistol

DECORATORS: pretty guns that are neither shooters nor valuable antiques

DETONATING POWDERS: also fulminating powders, fulminate of mercury

DOUBLE ACTION: pulling the trigger lines up a cartridge, cocks and fires the gun

DOUBLE GUN: either side-by-side or over-and-under rifle or shotgun

FIRE GILT: gold in mercury deposited on steel with heat. A poisonous process

FLASK: a container for gunpowder or priming powder

FLINTLOCK: gun or gunlock using flint and steel (Chapter 1)

FOWLER: smooth-bored long-barrel flintlock used for bird shooting

FRIZZEN (battery, steel): movable steel anvil on lock providing sparks

FURNITURE: the metal trimmings of a gun or pistol

GRIPS: left and right sides of a pistol "handle"

GROOVES: the valleys or channels in a rifled barrel

GUNPOWDER: any propelling charge—black, semismokeless, cordite, or smokeless

HAIR TRIGGER: a second trigger which lightens the pull of the real trigger

HALBERD: infantry weapon, spear, axe and hook on a pole

HAMMER: moving gun part that hits and explodes the primer

HAND CANNON: most primitive gun, a barrel on a stock without lock

HORSE PISTOL: large pistol used by cavalry

IGNITION SYSTEM: method of firing a gun (Chapter 1)

LANDS: the ridges in a rifled barrel

LEVER ACTION: magazine repeater worked by under lever

LOCK PLATE: metal to which lock parts —cock, frizzen, etc.—are attached

MAGNUM: designation of a hot or heavy load, especially .357, .44 revolver, .300 and .375 rifle

MANDREL: solid iron rod around which a barrel is formed

MARTIAL ARM: weapon designed for specific military use

MATCH CORD: twisted vegetable fibers soaked in saltpeter

MATCHLOCK: gun operated with a burning match cord held by a serpentine (Chapter 1)

MINIATURE: mechanically functioning arm made to diminutive scale

MINIE BALL: conical soft-lead bullet with a depression at the base

MINT: a gun in new condition

MIQUELET: Spanish-developed lock using flint, with exterior main spring (Chapter 1)

MUSKET: early, heavy matchlock requiring a fork: later, smoothbore infantry flintlock

NEEDLEFIRE: Dreyse's invention in which a needle in gun penetrates cartridge

NIPPLE: metal seat for percussion cap attached to gun barrel

PAN: metal tray under touch hole which holds priming powder

PATCH: small piece of greased cloth wrapped around bullet

PERCUSSION CAP: small copper cap which holds detonating material

PIN FIRE: early cartridge with a pin protruding from the base

PISTOL: can be used to designate a single shot, autoloading or machine (pistol)

PITTING: holes created by rust on the surface or bore of an arm

PRESENTATION (GUN): a gun with an inscription of gift to a person

PRIMING POWDER: finely ground black powder or (later) fulminating powder

PROOF MARK: city or state stamp on the barrel of gun proving it was tested by being shot

PROVENANCE: the previous ownership of an arm

PYRITES: iron disulfide, or fool's gold—used in wheel-lock ignition

RECEIVER: housing of the mechanism of a modern firearm

REGIMENTAL MARKINGS: stamps on stock, lock or barrel indicating army ownership

REVOLVER: multishot hand or long arm with revolving cylinder at barrel breech

RIFLE: long arm with grooves in the barrel to control bullet flight

ROLL ENGRAVING: design impressed mechanically with pressure

ROUND: a single shot

RUST: what gun collectors hate the most

SCURF: surface impurities worked out of steel billet by forging

SEAR: catch in gunlock holding hammer at half or full cock

SIDE PLATE: plate opposite lock, holding lock screws

SINGLE ACTION: revolver requiring manual cocking

SKELP: billet of iron used in forging gun barrels

SMOKELESS (POWDER): any of a variety of modern cartridge gun powders

SMOOTHBORE: designation of a shotgun, fowling piece or musket

SNAPHAUNCE: predecessor of true flintlock with separate steel and pan cover (Chapter 1)

SPANNER: wrench for winding the spring of a wheel lock

STEEL: frizzen or battery (q.v.)

STOCK: element of a gun, usually wood, which holds the lock and barrel

SUPERIMPOSED: system of loading more than one charge and ball in a single barrel

WHEEL LOCK: gun operated with a serrated steel wheel rubbing on pyrites (Chapter 1)

Types of Guns

HOW TO TELL A SNAPHAUNCE
FROM A SPENCER

Many a smart collector is a specialist, and as a specialist he knows more and more about less and less. Lots of collectors collect only Colts or only Winchesters or only wheel-lock pistols. I even know of two collectors who have narrowed their collecting interest to one model of the Colt revolver. Collectors Patterson and Barley of Pittsburgh own a joint collection of model 1851 Colt Navy percussion revolvers. They are not interested in 1861 Colts or 1849 pocket models — just 1851 Colt Navies. Another collector I know has a slightly broader interest. He collects everything Samuel Colt made in his lifetime, and at one time he owned most of the fine Colt Paterson pistols, Colt's first gun made in Paterson, New Jersey. This collector, however, has one weakness. He will collect anything that is legitimately collectible as long as it has the serial number 66. His name is Philip Phillips, of Phillips 66 Petroleum.

It doesn't matter how narrow your focus becomes when you are an advanced arms collector. In the beginning you will want to know as much as you can about all types of weaponry. You need to know what you are looking at whether you collect it or not. You will often pick up a bargain, not for your own collection but to trade it for something you want from another collector who isn't interested in cash.

There are broad categories of firearms which are easy to recognize at a glance. Knowing the type of gun will help you date it, determine the country where it was made, and give you a rough idea of its worth because of its rarity. There are nine major categories of firearms:

   (1) Hand cannon
   (2) Matchlocks
   (3) Wheel locks
   (4) Snaphaunces
   (5) Miquelet locks
   (6) Flintlocks
   (7) Transitional detonating
   (8) Percussion
   (9) Cartridge (this classification is the latest and most numerous)
       (a) Single shot
       (b) Revolver
       (c) Magazine repeater
       (d) Self-loader

Colt's Paterson revolver—Colt's first production gun made in Paterson, New Jersey, in the 1830s. This fine example in the Wadsworth Atheneum Collection in Hartford, Connecticut, has ten inlaid silver bands and ivory grips.

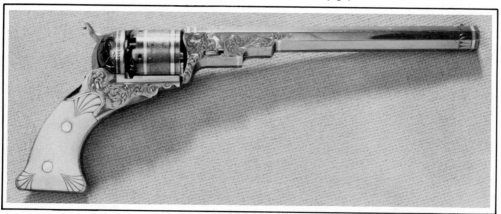

HAND CANNON

Hand cannon are a cinch to recognize. They have no mechanism to fire them. In order to shoot a hand cannon, you need a hot poker, a smouldering piece of punk or an ember from a fire. The hot thing, whatever it is, is brought to touch the hole in the breech of the gun where a little powder has been piled. The hot or burning punk or poker ignites the priming powder. This in turn shoots a flame down the touch hole and burns (explodes) the bigger charge in the barrel. This propelling charge pushes the bullet out of the barrel in one hell of a hurry, and that's what makes the hand cannon shoot.

Hand cannon are the simplest and oldest of all of the guns. The first pictures of hand cannon date back to the 1300s. The earliest surviving examples of hand cannon date only to the 1350s. Hand cannon vary greatly in size. Some are so big that while they can be carried by one man, they can only be shot by resting them on a support of some kind—a wall, a rock or the bulkhead of a ship. The bigger hand cannon are also called rampart guns or doppelhäcken (German for a double-sized gun with a hook on the bottom to catch against the wall to reduce recoil).

Smaller hand cannon vary in length from rifle size to pistol size. The Smithsonian Institution has a rifle-sized hand cannon which is actually rifled. It dates from the time of the Emperor Maximilian—the early 1500s—and has an identifying double-eagle coat-of-arms painted on either side of the slab-sided wooden stock. Other hand cannon have barrels no longer than a pistol. Some of these, from excavations in Switzerland, date from the early 1400s. Several are in the museum in Bern, Switzerland, but I know of one — in a private collection — which came from a flea market and cost only pennies, although it is about five hundred years old. Nothing was left but the barrel, and it looked like a piece of rusty pipe. The only way you could tell it was a gun was that the outside was half hexagonal and half round; the breech of the pipe was drilled to make a touch hole, and the barrel had been formed when hot by hammering over a mandrel and was not bored out or capped with a plug. You can tell this by cleaning the inside of the barrel and looking down the hole with a flashlight or one of those lights that dentists wear. The inside of the barrel of the breech will be cup-shaped where it was formed around the mandrel, not flat as if drilled and plugged.

All hand cannon are not as rare as the ones made in the 1400s in Europe. Hand cannon were made later in Africa, Afghanistan, India, and, most commonly, in China and the Philippines. These were made after the introduction of firearms by European sailors and traders. Some hand cannon were being made by primitive Philippino tribes in the outer islands as late as World War II, and for all I know, the Moros may still be making them out of water pipe liberated from the U.S. Army or the Japanese. In any event, it is possible to own an Oriental hand cannon for not too much money if you want to have a representative of each type of mechanism in your collection.

Hand cannon were extremely difficult to aim and shoot. You had to hold the gun with the left hand while you tried to poke the touch hole exactly in the center with a hot wire, poker or punk. This left you with no hands at all for aiming. If your were trying to shoot a hand cannon from horseback you were plumb out of luck. This simple problem led an unknown inventor to pin a little "S"-shaped hook onto the wooden side of the hand cannon stock so that the swinging hook part went in front of the touch hole. The hook held the punk,

Four-barrel hand cannon in the Winchester Gun Museum.

which was a piece of tree bark soaked in saltpeter and dried, or a wick, or "match," which was a twist of fibers similarly dunked and dried in the sun or by a fire. These inflammable starters were lit and continued to smoulder for a long time. When you wanted to shoot your gun, you blew hard on the punk, or "match," until it glowed. Then you pushed the metal holder up to where it could light the priming powder in order to fire the gun. You could do this with your thumb while holding the gun with both the left and right hand. This way it was possible to hold the gun with a firmer grip and even to aim it a little.

MATCHLOCK

A gun with a match holder attached is properly called a matchlock. There are different kinds of matchlock guns. The first and simplest has the metal match holder held to the gunstock by a nail, pin or screw. It is moved back and forth by hand. The metal holder is often in the form of an "S" or serpentine. The top of the "S" is split to hold the match or punk, the pin is in the middle of the "S," and the heavier bottom of the "S" serves as a balance which keeps the "S" match holder in an upright position until the shooter pushes the top part forward toward the touch hole to shoot the gun.

Improved matchlocks have springs and triggers added. Some models have springs which push against the holder to keep the hot match away from the touch hole until the shooter pushes against the spring or a trigger to shoot the gun. Other spring-loaded matchlock guns are called snap-match-locks. The snap-match serpentine is held back by a catch. When a pull on the trigger releases the catch, a spring pushes the serpentine holding the burning match to the touch hole. Careful adjustment of this type of mechanism is necessary so that the snap action does not extinguish the burning match.

From these simple methods of firing a gun, we come to the most complicated. Matchlock guns, which were used from some time in the 1400s until after 1700 by the European infantryman, were cheap to make, easy to repair and reasonably safe in the hands of the dumbest dogface. They had their drawbacks, however: they were slow to fire and they required a burning fire nearby to light the "match." A soldier on sentry duty had his hands full just keeping the match cord smouldering for however many hours he was on watch. When it rained, a matchlock gun was of as much use as a billy club. Whole battles were postponed by cloudbursts. The French and their Italian allies stood with rain running down their necks, unable to attack the Imperial Army of the Holy Roman Emperor at the battle of Pavia in 1515. Finally both sides quit and went home to get dried out and fight another day.

The worst thing about a matchlock gun was its smell and smoke. You had a hard time of it to surprise an enemy or a wild turkey when you had to tote a bonfire. If your were trying to hide out or lie in ambush for your opponent, the chances were that the smouldering match would give you away by the smell even if the fire was hidden by the trees. The English have an expression: "I smell a mouse." The expression that means the same thing in German is "I smell a match." This means the match of a hidden weapon.

Indian matchlock revolver from Colonel Colt's own collection, now in the Wadsworth Atheneum Collection in Hartford, Connecticut.

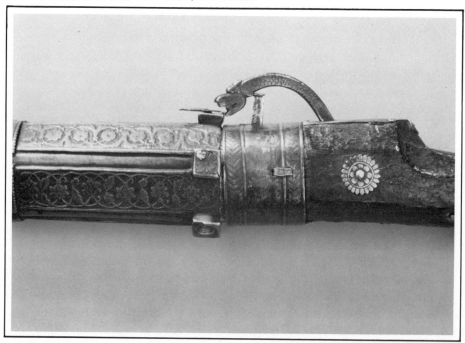

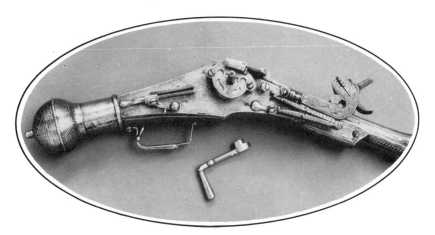

All metal Nuremberg wheel-lock pistol with a spanner, circa 1600, in the Metropolitan Museum of Art in New York, 14. 25. 1406A and 14. 25. 1520.

WHEEL LOCKS

With all the disadvantages of matchlocks, it was no wonder that in the late 1400s clock makers, who were the machinists of their day, looked around for a way to shoot a gun without a continuing burning fire. There was already a way to make a fire with a piece of flint and steel. Flint and steel struck together threw tiny particles of hot steel slivers into charred rags, called tinder, which started to smoulder. Blowing on these embers made them glow, and a regular fire could be started with bits of wood dipped in sulfur.

Need causes things to be invented. When a need is widely felt, often more than one person will invent the same thing at the same time. All we know is that the wheel-lock gun appeared at the end of the fifteenth century. Not surprising, the wheel-lock makers were often members of the families of watch and clock makers. The principle of the wheel-lock gunlock was well enough understood by around 1485 for Leonardo da Vinci to sketch the mechanism in his notebooks full of military inventions. Nobody knows today whether Leonardo should be called the inventor of the wheel-lock gun or its chronicler.

The wheel-lock lock has over forty parts. For all its complicated mechanism, it works like a Zippo cigarette lighter. The purpose of the machine is to throw a spark when you pull the trigger. With a Zippo, you simply spin a toothed steel wheel against a little piece of composite flint. The hot bits of steel hit the wick of the lighter and ignite the lighter fluid. The wheel lock works the same way. A spinning steel wheel with teeth rubs against a stone (iron pyrites, or fool's gold, a soft crumbly stone which won't wear out the steel wheel too fast), throwing hot steel sparks into a small pile of fine-ground gunpowder which ignites and fires the charge in the barrel. All this could be done with a hand crank or with your thumb, but then you could not take aim or think about anything else. That is where the invention came in. The European (Italian or German) clock makers of the fifteenth century made it possible to store up energy the same way you wind a clock or watch. A big heavy spring is cranked up tight with a separate key or wrench, called a spanner, and held under tension until you shoot the gun. When you pull on the trigger, you release the spring which zips the steel wheel around against the pyrites. The action is very fast. Pulling the trigger, the sparks, the primer flash, and the gun going off all seem to happen at once. Actually it takes place in a fraction of a second.

Wheel-lock guns were born complicated and grew worse. Springs were added to hold the pyrites firmly against the wheel. Another spring was added to push a cover over the priming pan to keep the powder from blowing away or getting wet. And, of course, there was a spring to keep the trigger forward against the pressure of the finger pull. Finally the wheel-lock makers added a series of leaf springs to make the trigger pull as light as a feather. An extra trigger was added to cock the hair-trigger mechanism. This is a simplified description of a single-shot wheel lock. They were more complicated when they were made to fire more than one shot or were self-spanning — that is, when they did not require being wound with a spanner, but cocked themselves when you brought the pyrites holding frizzen down to the wheel with your hand.

Not only were the wheel-lock guns expensive to make but they were so complicated that it took a skilled gunsmith mechanic to make or repair them. They were also a bit delicate because of the number of parts which could get out of order. For these reasons, the wheel-lock gun never did become the weapon of the common foot soldier. It was carried by officers and by heavy cavalry. The matchlock gun, with all its disadvantages, stayed in military use until long after another invention, the flintlock, made its replacement possible.

THE SNAPHAUNCE

The flintlock was the product of a process of development. There was an obvious need for a simpler, cheaper gun-firing mechanism than the wheel lock. The first thing to be eliminated was the wheel itself. A lot of moving parts were saved by replacing the steel wheel with a grooved or smooth steel plate against which a stone — either pyrites or flint, which is harder—could be slammed by a spring. The inside mechanism remained similar to the wheel lock and the spark-producing steel was one piece, while the sliding pan cover which protected the priming powder was separate. This gun, almost as old as the wheel lock, is called the snaphaunce. It was developed by German or Dutch gunsmiths perhaps as early as 1540. The name

Pair of Brescian snaphaunce pistols with cut steel stock inlays and sculptured monsters in steel forming the cocks and batteries. Victoria and Albert Museum Nos. 2242 and 2242A — 1855. These pistols were made about 1645, signed Lazarino Cominazo.

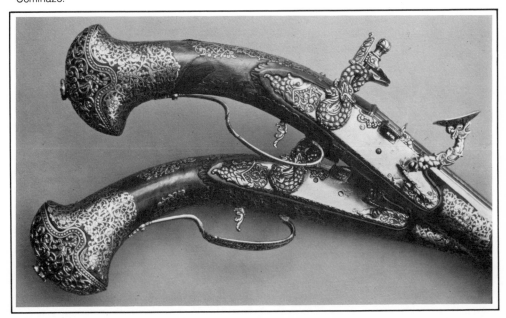

snaphaunce (a pecking hen in Dutch or Low German) describes the action of the cock holding the flint dipping forward to strike the steel or battery much as a chicken would bend over and strike its head forward to seize a grain of corn. For a long time the name was given a romantic but wrong attribution: historians said the gun was invented by Dutch chicken thieves who couldn't afford wheel locks. Actually some of the snaphaunce guns were rather fancy, with fine engraving and inlay work. Some Dutch snaphaunce guns were taken to Russia by Peter the Great, who, as a boy, had learned shipbuilding and other trades in Holland in the late 1600s. The Russians, however, had known about snaphaunces for a long time and had been building their own versions early in the century. In Italy, the snaphaunce system is known as *ala fiorentina* (the Florentine system). Snaphaunces lasted longest in Italy, where they were still being built as late as 1810.

MIQUELET LOCKS

Another attempt to beat the high cost and difficult manufacture of the wheel lock was the Spanish miquelet. The name miquelet also has a romantic connection. The "miquelets" were Spanish bandits who were sort of a combination of Robin Hoods and Don Quixotes; they lived in the mountain passes, robbed the rich and gave to the poor. In reality, however, it was the gunsmiths in the town of Ripoli and the cities of Barcelona and Madrid who simplified the wheel lock,

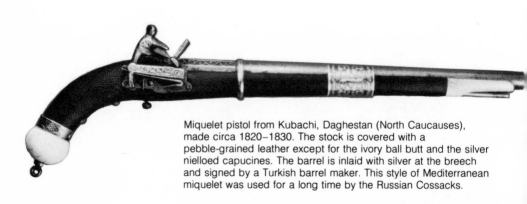

Miquelet pistol from Kubachi, Daghestan (North Caucauses), made circa 1820–1830. The stock is covered with a pebble-grained leather except for the ivory ball butt and the silver nielloed capucines. The barrel is inlaid with silver at the breech and signed by a Turkish barrel maker. This style of Mediterranean miquelet was used for a long time by the Russian Cossacks.

which had been brought to Spain by Charles V in the 1530s. The miquelet combined the steel with the primer-pan cover, making an "L"-shaped piece. This was efficiency. When the flint hit the steel it not only threw sparks but it opened the lid to the primer pan which was protected until the second of firing. The miquelet can be identified by its big springs on the outside of the lock and by the deep grooves in the steel or battery. There is little mechanism on the inside of a miquelet lock. The cock is held at full and half cock by pins which stick out through holes in the lock plate operating laterally.

Since the kings of Spain were also kings of Naples for a long time, the Spanish miquelet lock was made not only in Naples but in other parts of Italy, where it was called the *systema ala Romano*. The miquelet locks are simple and strong. If the springs break, they are easy to replace. The steel is deeply grooved and often has a replaceable striking face held to the battery by a lock screw. These miquelet guns and pistols were copied by all of the countries bordering the Mediterranean. North African, Syrian, Turkish and Albanian copies are more common than the Spanish originals and not usually as well made. The popularity of the system even reached the south of Russia by way of the Bosphorus and the Black Sea. In Algieria and Tunisia crude miquelet guns and pistols are still being made for the tourist trade.

FLINTLOCKS

Both the snaphaunce and the miquelet had elements which were used in the invention of the flintlock. This may not have been by any evolutionary process but simply a similar response to the same set of circumstances. There was a need for a simpler, cheaper, easier-to-make and maintain gunlock. The flintlock is sometimes called the French lock because it was invented in the early years of the seventeenth century by gunsmiths who worked for the kings of France.

Louis XIII of France was a gun nut who owned seven wheel locks when he was ten years old. When he was thirteen he owned fifty. Before he died, he owned two hundred fifty and was known as Louis the Gunsmith (Louis l'Arquebusier). One of the artisans who built

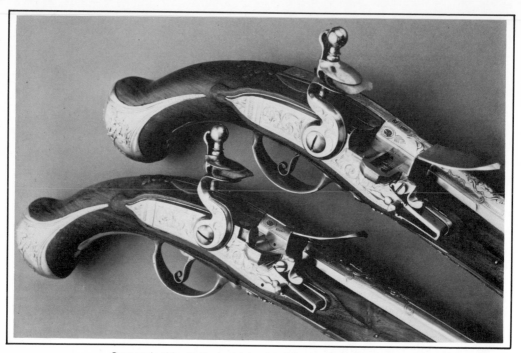

Over-and-under flintlock pistols of polished etched steel and gold on brass. These are from the collection of the Grand Duke of Saxe Weimar, now in the Tower of London, XII 1556, 1557. They are in powder puff condition with gold inlaid stamps at the breech. The rear sight is the bust of a woman, also gilt.

guns for the king was the watchmaker Marin le Bourgeoys. He and his brothers made guns, clocks and machines to demonstrate the movements of the sun, moon and stars for Louis XIII (reigned 1610-1643) and his father before him. Sometime after 1600 Marin made a big flintlock gun for the father, Henri IV. This gun still survives, in a museum in Leningrad. A few years later Marin's brother, Pierre, made a second flintlock gun. This one is much smaller since it was made for the boy-king, Louis. It, too, survives and can be seen in the Metropolitan Museum of Art in New York.

The flintlock uses elements found on both the snaphaunce and the miquelet locks. The flintlock steel is combined with the priming-pan cover into one piece of steel. The cock, which holds a piece of flint, comes forward and strikes the steel, throwing sparks into the just-opened pan. Cock and half cock are accomplished with notches cut in a vertically operating wheel on the inside of the lock which is attached to the cock. This is true flintlock. It was so successful that within a few years it graduated from being a royal plaything to become a weapon issued to the army to replace the matchlock. Military examples of the flintlock were being made by the Bourgeoys or by their contemporaries. The flintlock gun worked so well that it was adopted by all of the European nations and was the standard military weapon until the 1830s and '40s, even though detonating powders had been invented thirty years before.

TRANSITIONAL DETONATORS

Flintlock guns were the standard weapon until 1806, when a Scottish Presbyterian minister, the Reverend Alexander Forsyth, applied one of the new developments in chemistry, detonating powders, to firearms. The new powders exploded when they were hit with a hammer. The spark-producing flint or pyrites were not needed. For several years after the Reverend Forsyth's application many mechanical devices were invented to hold the powders. These were made after 1806 for about twenty years. All of them are collector's pieces today. The first system, Forsyth's, used a metal bottle on a pivot, which spilled out a little of primer powder when it was tipped.

Other transitional detonating systems included pills made of the powders and pill holders to hold the pills while they were being hit by the hammer. There were pellets which were magazine-fed onto an anvil, and there were little copper tubes, like straws, which were fed into the touch hole and exploded by squeezing the tube.

Transitional five-barrel gun. This Forsyth "Detonator" was the first to use percussion powders. The scent-bottle-shaped primer mechanism released a small quantity of percussion powder when it was rotated. Circa 1820, London Tower XII 1589.

PERCUSSION

The first percussion caps were made by an English artist, Joshua Shaw, in 1816. Shaw came to Philadelphia in 1817 and patented his invention in 1822. The copper cap filled with detonating fulminate which fitted over a nipple screwed into the end of the touch hole became the standard way to fire a gun. By the late 1820s all other systems were obsolete and had been replaced, although armies of the world also kept on using up their old flintlocks.

In the United States the percussion musket and percussion revolver were the standard weapons all through the Civil War, even though cartridge guns had been invented.

CARTRIDGES

The French gun designers—Pauly in 1812, Robert, LeFaucheux and Flobert during the early and middle 1800s—made different types of self-contained cartridges and guns to shoot them. These cartridges contained a priming charge, a propelling charge and a bullet, no matter what system they employed. Pin fire was the most popular in Europe but never caught on in America.

In the late 1850s dozens of American inventors wanted to cash in on the growing need for guns both for the West and for the impending Civil War. The most successful were Spencer and Winchester, but if you collect guns of the Civil War period you will learn to recognize over fifty different makers.

SINGLE SHOT

Single-shot cartridge guns are still being made for target shooting and sometimes for hunters who are sure of themselves. The first single-shot cartridge guns to be adopted by the armies were the German Dreyse, a needle-fired gun, the French Chassepot and the British Snyder, which was invented by an American from Brooklyn. In the United States, single-shot rifles were made in Providence,

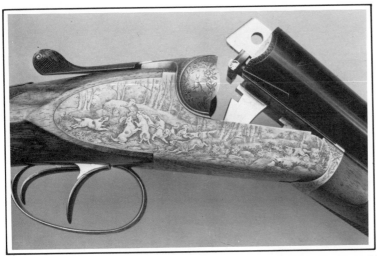

Modern cartridge shotgun with sidelocks fully engraved with all-over scene of fox hunting. Made by August Francotte in the early years of the twentieth century. Musée d'Armes V23 Ao56/5445.

Rhode Island, by Peabody; by Remington in Illion, New York; by the Springfield arsenal; Ballard; Maynard; Sharps; Stevens; Frank Wesson and Whitney, to mention a few. Many of these old guns will shoot right along with new guns if they have been well treated.

REVOLVER

Colt's percussion revolver had been a great success, but the cartridge revolver, originally patented by Smith & Wesson, made arms history. Cartridge revolvers firing from five to nine shots are still the most popular and positive kind of handgun in America.

MAGAZINE REPEATER

America is particularly famous for having invented the magazine repeater. The brands one thinks of first, Marlin and Winchester, are still being made today, but at the time of the Civil War it was young Christopher Spencer who caught the popular imagination. Spencer

Gauvain of Paris made this fine percussion revolver after the middle of the nineteenth century. Two female figures ride the hammer while an old man holds his ears against the percussion blast. From the Charles Noë Daly collection now in the Metropolitan Museum of Art, No. 35.81.4.

One of the earliest revolver mechanisms. This beautifully decorated wheel-lock revolver has a gilt lattice over the blued cylinder with the royal Austrian coat of arms. It dates from around 1590–1600, 240 years before Colt. Kunsthistorisches Museum, Vienna, No. A 1145.

was only twenty when the war started. He went to work and invented a repeating rifle which fed cartridges through a tube in the shoulder stock. Nobody in Washington paid any attention to him because of his youth until one day he saw Lincoln on the White House lawn. He told Mr. Lincoln his story, and Lincoln gave him a chance to demonstrate his invention. The two of them shot Spencer's gun in back of the White House and Spencer went home with an order. He built ninety thousand rifles for the Union during the war.

SELF-LOADER

After you shoot a magazine repeater you have to cock the gun for the next shot. A more recent invention does this for you. It is called a self-loader. The self-loading gun works on a variety of principles. Some are spring-operated and some work with the pressure of the gas which escapes when the gun is fired. All of them, one way or another, use some of the energy of the first cartridge to get rid of the used-up case and to place the next cartridge in firing position. The first self-loader was invented by Hugo Borchardt in 1893. The Bergmann, the Luger and the Mauser followed in quick succession, but the all-time winner was the Browning "Automatic." Browning self-loaders have been made since 1900 by Colt, Winchester, Remington and the biggest arms factory in the world, the Fabrique National in Liège, Belgium. The most famous is the Colt 45, which was used by the United States Army in two world wars.

In order to understand more about the different types of guns, you must know about all of the different parts which go into a single finished gun and what it takes to make a gun work. A matchlock is no good without a match; a wheel lock without the spanner; a modern cartridge gun without the ammunition. This will be explored next.

Parts
and Accessories

WHAT BITS GO WITH WHAT PIECES

All the machines you see around you today, from house jacks to automobiles, owe their beginnings to the metalworkers of the Middle Ages. These stubborn craftsmen learned by trial and error how to temper a sword blade hard enough to hold a razor edge and yet flexible enough to bend and not break. They learned to take raw iron ore and work it with heat and hammer to make armor. It had to be soft enough to flow under the hammer's blows from a block of iron into a graceful helmet of steel, the crown or skull all one piece of metal. Then the armor, after being hammered into shape and filed smooth and etched with decoration, was made hard enough on the surface to turn the blade of the sharpest sword or arrowhead.

The most difficult job of all was saved for the gunsmiths. Not one, but half a dozen different kinds of steel were required to make one gun. The steel in the barrel had to be stretchy, malleable, so that it wouldn't shatter like glass under the impact of the explosion. Very soft iron or mild steel was no good either because the soft metal would wear out too quickly from the friction of the bullet going through the barrel. The hammers or cocks of flint guns had to be tough so that they wouldn't crystallize and break from being struck. The steels or frizzens of flintlocks, or the steel wheels of wheel locks, had to be as glass hard so that the flint of pyrites would rub off sparks. Springs are the hardest, since each requires special tempering, depending on its job and the distance it had to travel. Other parts such as the lock plate, the fittings or furniture did not present such problems, but the hand-filed screws had to be made of the right material or they would break off in the screw holes and ruin the gun.

BARRELS

From the day guns were invented, barrels have been a problem for the gunsmith. The ancient gunsmiths tried to make barrels out of flat strips of iron or staves. They would weld these together around an iron rod, or mandrel. Since the weld was primitive and not guaranteed to hold, the barrel was reinforced with cherry-hot iron bands driven over the barrel made of staves and allowed to cool and shrink. As the barrelmaker-gunsmiths became more expert they learned to control their heat and they also learned how to make iron more ductile by heat and hammering. Spanish gunsmiths made excellent gun barrels out of old horseshoes and even horseshoe nails. They let the horses do part of the hammering just having them walk shod on cobblestone pavement. These bits of iron were first forged into shovel-shaped pieces. Five or six of them would be forged into one seamless tube around an iron rod, or mandrel, the size of the eventual bore. Only much later was it possible for a gunsmith to find a piece of steel big enough, and with the right "stretch," that he could drill out and rifle for a gun barrel.

All that survives from the earliest guns are the barrels. The wooden stocks have long since rotted to nothing, and the smaller fittings have rusted, been broken or lost. Well-made early barrels are collected and exhibited in museums and private collections as examples of skilled metal work. Sometimes the old barrels are restocked with modern wood to show how the original gun looked.

Later barrels are also collector's pieces, especially when they are

Elkhorn priming powder flask finely engraved with a Diana? Brunhilda? a devil, a lobster and rococo designs, silver caps and pouring spout, circa 1620. The inscribed legend is in both Latin and German. It says "Infortunium" and translates "Das Ungluck."

decorated with engraving or inlay of brass, copper, gold and silver. The name of the maker engraved or stamped or inlaid on a gun barrel, as well as the workmanship, can make it a valuable item to collect.

Many historically minded collectors haunt old battlefields with metal detection devices. When they find a buried weapon, about all they are able to excavate is a rusty barrel and an odd-shaped chunk of rust that was once a lock. The same is true of "finds" from sunken ships. If the iron survives at all, as it may if discovered in fresh water, little of the wooden part of the stock will be left and that will crumble once it is exposed to the air. Excavated weapons, however, are all we have to go by to study some remote periods and some not so remote. For example, in 1745 the English forbade the Scots any potentially lethal weapon. This was a weapon law to end all weapon laws. Any Scot caught with a gun was shot where he stood. He got no trial, no nothin'. Thus there are virtually no guns surviving from Scotland from before 1745 except those that were buried in the dead of night and excavated years later when the heat died down.

If you collect Scottish pistols, you don't object to a little pitting from rust around the barrels.

LOCKS

Many a collector will have a drawer or a case full of gunlocks. These complicated pieces of machinery can tell us much about history and the advance of technology. Early locks, especially wheel locks, can be masterpieces of handwork. Not only the lock plates, which everyone could see were engraved, etched, inlaid and sometimes gilded, but the inside of the locks were often decorated with engraving. This work was expected to be seen only by another locksmith, something like the work of the Gothic stone sculptors who carved gargoyles and devils on the spires of cathedrals where they could only be seen by God or low-flying angels.

Locks and receivers of the eighteenth, nineteenth and the present century are found in study collections of museums. By comparing one lock with another it is possible to see the advance of the gunmakers' logic. The weaknesses in the engineering of the Volcanic can be seen in comparison with the Henry and the first Winchester '66. In turn, the mechanism of the '66 is strengthened and refined successively in the Winchester models of 1873, 1876 and 1886. The differences in the receivers of these guns, while slight to a novice, are instantly obvious to a Winchester collector.

The inside of the lock of a breech-loading, cartridge, wheel-lock gun in the Russell Aitken Collection. The inside of the lock, which was probably never seen by the owner, is engraved with monsters, sea serpents, a bird-headed dragon, and a rabbit eating the tip of a carrot.

"Furniture"

Even the decoration of the finer handmade early guns is collectable. The grotesque masks on flintlock pistols and the panoplies of arms on all sorts of guns make attractive tie clasps and cuff links. Of course, nobody is going to pry off a part of a good gun to make a tie clasp or a bolo knot, but odd parts do turn up and recasts can be made. I have a pair of cuff links made from a cast of an old man's face on the butt of George Washington's flintlock pistols at West Point!

Powder Flasks

In addition to parts of guns, many attractive accessories are often more rare and sometimes more valuable than the weapons themselves. There are many powder-flask collectors who collect flasks of all periods. Flasks have been made out of every known material including turtle shells, ivory, iron, wood, gourds, elk horn, bone, cowhorn, brass, mother-of-pearl, gold, silver and even coconut shells. Benvenuto Cellini is supposed to have worked on some, and many a fine goldsmith and ivory carver has done his best work decorating powder flasks.

Some of the earliest flasks were made of iron and were combination tools. A flask dating from the mid-sixteenth century is in the Charles Addams collection and another, in the Palazzo Ducale museum in Venice, is shaped like a narrow ice cream cone. The cone part holds the gunpowder. At the small end are four socket wrenches for spanning wheel-lock guns of different sizes and at the larger, "ice cream," end is a screwdriver. The iron shell shows traces of fire gilding in a tracery design.

While this is one of the earliest flasks I have ever seen, many beautiful ones survive from the wheel lock, matchlock period. I was in my dentist's chair having my teeth cleaned one day when the dentist asked me if all flasks were made of cowhorn. After I spit out the gargle, I asked him what prompted the question. He said that he had seen a big, flat flask with an iron spout engraved on the side with a sixteenth-century soldier in a slashed uniform. The flask was in the

A detached sculptured and gold inlaid pistol
barrel dating from the 1660s. It is possibly the
work of Adrian Reynier (le Hollandois), a master
Liège gunsmith who worked in Paris. From the
van Zuylen Collection

Adam and Eve flask of sculptured ivory against a
brown field. The metal fittings are gilt bronze. The
back of the flask is solid ivory with the Welsperg
coat of arms. Victoria and Albert Museum
234-1854.

window of a thriftshop across the street, and the lady who ran the thriftshop didn't know what it was. The dentist had to tie me to the chair to finish the teeth cleaning. Five minutes after I left his office I owned a fine Dutch powder flask which had been used by a musketeer with a matchlock in the days of D'Artagnan.

Some of the finer horn and ivory flasks are carved in full relief with game animals, beautiful maidens or gods and heros from classical mythology. An ivory flask as big as a pie-sized doughnut carved with deer, elk, boar, rabbits and hounds is in the museum in Munich, Germany; another, which, though hundreds of years old, looks like it was just carved out of whipped cream, is preserved in a private collection in New York.

One day in a little town in central Pennsylvania I saw a flask combined with a bullet bag for the powder and ball for a Tschincke, or wheel-lock small-bore rabbit or squirrel gun, which I owned. The flask was decorated with scratch engraving of figures of hunters and dots and circles cut in the bone or horn and filled in with brown and greenish inks. I tried to buy the flask, but the dealer knew what he had and was asking as much for the flask as my gun was worth.

Some of the most popular flasks collected in the United States are the engraved cowhorn flasks carried by the frontiersmen and early settlers. A few of these date back to the French and Indian Wars in the 1760s and were engraved with maps of early settlements and travel routes, such as the city of Philadelphia or the forts along the Hudson River Valley. The flask most often carried by the Kentucky rifleman was a cowhorn flask tied over his shoulder with a piece of rawhide. Often the flask was made by the rifleman and would have engraved on it, in rough characters, his name, the date, and possibly a hunting or battle scene he knew first hand.

The other popular flasks to collect are the brass, zinc and copper flasks of the nineteenth century used during the percussion period. Colt supplied a number of them to go with the Colt percussion revolver. If you are lucky, you will find them in cases with Colt pistols and screwdrivers, ramrods, capping tools and extra cylinders.

For more than a century, Dixon of Edinburg has been making fine brass flasks and they still make them for modern cap-and-ball shooters. You can buy these from Dixie Gun Works, Numerich, Navy Arms, and others. These flasks are made in the same way they always have been. Each half is stamped out separately in its gourd shape and decorated with embossed hunting scenes, panoplies of arms, or crossed American flags. The two halves are soldered together and a pouring spout and measure are threaded and screwed into the top of the flask. There are many designs to choose from, and the older Colt flasks are quite desirable and valuable.

The best flask I ever saw, I traded for seven other flasks I owned and in turn traded for a fine pair of French flintlock pistols and a round ivory wheel-lock flask with carved boar and deer. This remarkable flask was on a trader's table with a pile of junk at a gun show in Williamsburg. The flask caught my eye because it was made of gracefully shaped panels of engraved mother-of-pearl held together in a framework of gold ormolu. The whole piece was very delicate and reflected light in all directions. I got the piece for the seven more ordinary flasks which I owned and then started to trace its ancestry. There was a picture of the flask in gun dealer Ray Riling's *The Powder Flask Book*. From this book I learned that the flask, number 1222-2, had come from the French court of the mid-eighteenth century. It was much too delicate and handsome to go with anything in my collection so I traded it to an advanced collector for a pair of silver wire inlaid flintlock pistols by Fatou of Paris and a little German ivory flask which matched a matchlock gun I owned.

ETCETERA

All kinds of powder measures, antique bullet molds, patch cutters, screwdrivers, nipple wrenches and fitted cases once discarded by collectors are now highly prized. One of the greatest American collectors of all times, William Renwick, used to discard the cases that his cased Colts had come in from the factory. Today the original cases are worth almost as much as the revolver, and a revolver in a case with its tools and spare parts is worth twice as much as the pistol by itself. The great Remington collector Carl Moldenhauer is especially happy when he can find a Remington pistol in the original cardboard box in which it was sold.

Powder testers, gunmakers tools, big wooden rifling machines which were turned by hand, are all highly desirable additions to your collection, and, I might add, not easy to come by. Not everyone knows what they are, so keep your eyes peeled when you go to a junk shop or a second hand store.

Tinder lighter with pistol mechanisms and even the simpler flint and steel, both of which preceded our present-day safety matches, used to be found in antique shops for five or ten dollars. They can still be found in antique shops but the price has gone up. Keep your eye out for a truly rare combination—a flintlock pistol tinder lighter which is also convertible into a shooting flintlock pistol. One of these, in good condition, is worth several thousand dollars.

Back in the days of flintlock and wheel-lock guns, it took a lot of equipment to shoot a gun. Look at the musketeer in the 1606 picture of

Collection of nineteenth-century powder flasks, bullet pouches, powder measure, bullet mould, spring compressor, and nipple wrench.

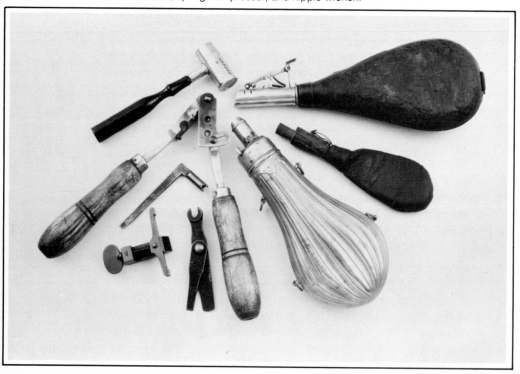

deGheyn and you will see what the soldier had to carry: a bullet pouch, a hank of match cord, a priming powder flask, a bandoleer with the twelve disciples (twelve premeasured charges of black powder in wooden tubes suspended on the strap), not to mention his musket, a musket rest and his fighting sword, usually a heavy rapier. If the soldier were carrying a caliver instead of a musket, he would have been carrying a big iron- or brass-bound powder flask instead of the bandoleer. In addition, each infantryman probably wore an iron bulletproof vest or cuirass under his blouse and, if not a pot helmet, an iron liner under his felt hat. All these accessories are collectible and very desirable.

I found a whole bandoleer and a hank of match cord in the attic of an old house. Individual powder-charge holders made of wood, metal or ivory often turn up. Rarer are the flasks and still rarer are the little boxes, called patrons, which hunters and target shooters used to carry. These held four, five or six paper cartridges consisting of a lead ball and a powder charge wrapped and tied up in a twist of paper for ease and speed in loading a muzzle-loading gun.

Spanners and Wrenches

Wheel-lock spanners, the wrenches used to wind up the main spring of the wheel-lock guns, come in all sizes and shapes. Some of them are simple tools such as you might find in any tool chest. (You can span a wheel lock with a modern socket wrench, but don't try, you might just break the old mainspring.) Other spanners have ivory handles. Some are combined with other tools such as an adjustable priming-powder measure and are very ingenious. Still others are carved steel and gilt and inlaid. These are not-so-minor works of art and are often finished to match the wheel-lock guns which belonged to a prince's hunting set. Sometimes these sets were given as wedding presents, others were coronation gifts made especially for the occasion, and the guns and the spanners were decorated with the coat of arms and the monograms of the people concerned. Often these spanners, being small, were lost, while the gun or set of guns were kept. This makes the spanners all the more valuable when they turn up.

CARTRIDGES

Cartridge collectors live in a world apart. When you stop to think that for every gun that was ever invented there must be at least half a dozen possible different loads that can be shot in it, you begin to realize how many cartridges it takes to make up a collection. Only a few lucky collectors can ever hope to own the complete cartridge-making kit that went with the first cartridge gun invented by Pauly, but practically every one living in the eastern half of the United States can start a cartridge collection with a minie ball from a Civil War battlefield. Pin-fire and needle-fire cartridges are odd-ball types which are not too hard to come by; rim-fire 41 pistol and 41 Swiss rifle cartridges, the long, skinny velo-dog from the age of bicycles and the huge 8-bore nitro express elephant cartridges can be found with a little digging and will add interest to your collection.

The subtleties of cartridge collecting are too complex and too numerous for this book on gun collecting. There are several good books devoted entirely to cartridge collecting, including Herschel Logan's *Cartridges*, reprinted by Bonanza. In addition, there is such a wide interest in cartridge collecting that Frank Wheeler averages eight pages of pictures and text in his monthly article in *The Gun Report* called "The Cartridge Collector." Besides reporting on odd-ball cartridges and unusual boxes that they come in, Wheeler's columns list the collectors get-togethers . . . "The Kansas Cartridge Collector's Association held their Annual Official Meeting on Saturday, January 19 at . . . "

Collecting cartridges or wheel-lock spanners may be a bit too specialized for your interest, but everyone will want to take a look at the weapons that relate to American history.

Guns Used In America

DID COLUMBUS HAVE A FLINTLOCK?
WHY DID JOHN PAUL JONES WEAR FIVE PISTOLS
IN HIS BELT?

Since America was discovered back in the days of hand cannon, every kind of mechanism and every type of gun has seen service in the Americas. The history of the invention of firearms is closely tied to the history of the discovery and exploration of the new continents. Without guns, the Conquistadores, more than likely, might still be fighting the Aztecs and the Incas. The English, Dutch and French colonists of North America might still be pinned to coastal settlements, huddling in mortal terror of Indian raids. Guns made all the difference in the exploration and development of the New World, even though their initial impact was more psychological than physical.

If Leif Ericson or Eric the Red did indeed reach the New World in their long, open boats, they did not have the protection of firearms. In A.D. 1000, gunpowder was still a hundred and fifty years away from being described by Roger Bacon in cabalistic double talk. Anyway their powder would have been too wet to use against the Indians they supposedly met at their landings in Newfoundland and on the Elizabeth Islands south of Providence, Rhode Island. They probably did land. Historian Samuel Eliot Morison is able to point out foundation stones of their sheds or houses along the Canadian Atlantic shore. The fact that they did not stick around may be attributed to their fear of the unknown number of savages who might descend on their settlements in the dead of night.

HAND CANNON

Columbus, Balboa and Cortés all had guns. The shoulder-held hand cannon weren't of much use against the Indians. You would have to catch the Indian first and tie him down in order to hit him with an arquebus, either hand cannon or matchlock. Wheel-lock guns had just been invented, but because of their expense were never in common use by the infantry and were rare everywhere until the last quarter of the 1500s. Nonetheless, guns played their part. The Spanish, splendid in their polished steel armor, fired off volleys of charges from their arquebuses. This impressed the Indians no end. Where did the thunder and lightning and smoke come from? These men must be some sort of gods. The Spanish took full advantage of the psychological effect and let go with a volley whenever their image seemed to be slipping. Coronado took the precaution of hauling a number of small cannon with him from lower California all the way across the great American desert to Great Bend, Kansas. There weren't any targets worthy of shooting at with cannon, but every once in a while Coronado would have his artillery captain fire off a salute just to show who was boss. The candle really wasn't worth the game, and one by one the cannon were lost in gullies and at river crossings by the sweaty, weary soldiers who had to drag the little monsters over the broiling prairies.

The real military uselessness of the original handguns was pointed out by both the Spanish and the English soldier-adventurers. Cabeza da Vaca describes in agonizing detail the misery of being shot at by the Seminole Indians, and being hit and wounded with reed arrows which penetrated the chinks of his armor. He tells of being shot six or seven times by Indians in ambush while he was trying to load his arquebus for a single shot. Captain John Smith in the early 1600s reported back to his bosses in London, the Virginia Company financiers, that the matchlock guns which had been issued to the settlers were useless against Indian attack. His report ended with a plea, "Please send firelocks" which was the old word for wheel locks. Up until now we did not know whether Captain Smith's plea was answered. Recently the National Park Service, under the direction of their Chief Historian, Harold L. Peterson, has identified the rusty remains of wheel-lock locks that have been excavated in the neighborhood of the original Virginia settlement at Jamestown.

WHEEL LOCKS

We know from another source the value the English sea dogs put on their wheel-lock firearms. Martin Frobisher and a number of his contemporaries had portraits of themselves painted while they held in their right hands what was undoubtedly one of their most valued possessions, an imported wheel-lock pistol.

The coast of Northern Florida and the offshore islands of the West Indies are littered with the barrels of Spanish, Dutch, French and English cannon used in the incessant wars for possession of the colonial empire, but there are very few handguns. The tropic heat and damp have disintegrated what must have been thousands of wheel locks and Spanish miquelet guns and pistols brought to the New World. Guns sunk with the Spanish treasure ships have fared no better. The iron locks and barrels didn't have a chance against the corrosive action of salt water. Only occasionally does a brass barrel of a pistol or the silver furniture from an officer's piece break the surface in a deep-sea diver's basket.

MATCHLOCKS

When the Pilgrim Fathers landed in Massachusetts Bay and the Dutch settled in New Amsterdam the soldiers who guarded the infant colonies were armed with matchlock muskets. While they were of limited use against a dancing, disappearing savage, the European soldiers did the best that they could. They stood sentry duty with their muskets at the ready. The match cord was lit at both ends so that if one smouldering tip went out they still had the other. Their guns were loaded and primed and they had extra powder in their flasks and often kept a couple of lead bullets in their mouths, since their hands were busy with their muskets and burning match cords. You or I couldn't hit the broad side of a barn with one of these clumsy rigs, but it is amazing what the old soldiers could do when their lives depended on it. They learned to shoot ducks and turkeys with these arquebuses and calivers, although most, if not all, of their bird shooting was done while the bird was on the ground. They even taught the Indians how to shoot. That was a mistake. While the Indians were more skilled in the woods and could sneak silently up on wild game until they were close enough for a sucker shot, they could do the same to a white colonist. This the settlers learned to their dismay when the Indians massacred the whites at the beginning of King Philip's War.

At first, wherever the white men landed, the native Indians were impressed by the noise and flash of the guns, but all too soon the newly arrived Europeans would decide that it was a good idea to arm the natives to fight against another group of settlers. The French did it and so did the English and both suffered from their shortsightedness. The Indians suffered the most, as the whites conveniently forgot who had armed the aborigines and proceeded to massacre and exterminate them for their savagery.

By the late 1600s the new flintlock guns were making an appearance in the New World. They made a lot of sense here and were immediately in great demand. The matchlocks were too slow and clumsy for hunting or fighting in the forest and the few wheel-lock guns were not only too expensive for most of the colonists but they were almost impossible to repair, given the limited skills and tools of the frontier blacksmith. The flintlock, on the other hand, was positive. It shot quickly, and the local blacksmith could make a new mainspring if the old one broke.

Flintlock guns made the advance of colonization, exploration and inland settlement possible. Every male citizen carried a loaded flint-

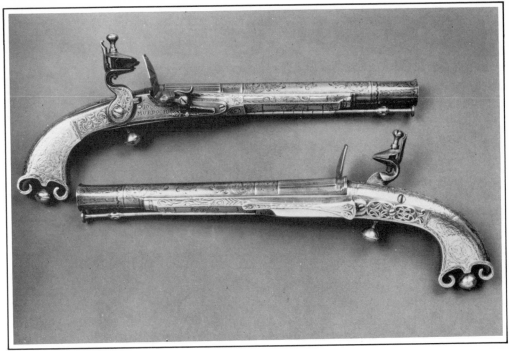

All metal Scottish pistols signed Io. (John) Murdock Doun. The stocks are silver and the barrels, cocks, locks, and stocks are engraved. Not-so-fancy Scotch pistols as these were carried by Scottish regimental troops in both the French and Indian and the Revolutionary Wars. Joe Kindig Collection.

lock gun or rifle. It was protection against thieves and Indians and it provided dinner. A gun, a knife, an axe and a plowshare were the most important possessions of the families who broke the virgin soil and built America.

MILITARY MUSKETS

The early flintlock guns in North America came in three styles. The first was the military musket. It was a sturdy piece with a full-length stock, swivels attached to the stock for shoulder sling, and a lump or lug on the end of the barrel for the attachment of a bayonet. The military muskets had heavy, smooth-bored long barrels. The English Brown Bess in the early 1700s had a 46-inch barrel, and its French counterpart, called the Charleville, was almost as long and

Boston club or sow-belly-stocked fowling piece signed on the lock "Richards." The lock was probably made in London between 1700 a d 1730 by Thomas Richards. The slightly bell-mouthed fowler is in the collection of Howard Greene, No. 230.

Brown Bess made up in the U.S. with a banana-shaped lock signed "Wilson/London" and surcharged "U.S." The stock is branded in several places "United States/ U.S./ U. States." The flintlock musket was carried by Continental soldier Samuel Stratton in the Battle of Long Island. The arm saw service in three wars. Howard Greene Collection No. 358.

heavy. The musket was an all-purpose gun. With a round ball it was a military weapon which could be used equally effectively in hunting deer or bear. For smaller game, the same gun was loaded with large "swan shot," or lead pellets smaller than BB's, depending on whether the quarry was a turkey or a dove.

HUDSON VALLEY FOWLERS

The all-purpose musket was supplemented by better, specialized weapons for hunting. The English brought with them long, light and graceful guns which they had used back home for water fowling. These guns were built here and evolved into what we call the Hudson Valley fowler. Many of these guns were, to be sure, built along the banks of the Hudson River, but an equal or even a greater number were made in New England and along the banks of the Potomac and the Chesapeake.

KENTUCKY RIFLES

The German and Swiss settlers who funneled through the port of Philadelphia to settle in central Pennsylvania and Maryland brought with them their native hunting weapons. These were short, heavy-barrel, big-bore Scheutzen rifles, great for accurate shooting a deer and boar in the mountains of Switzerland and in the Black Forest of Germany. The Swiss and German immigrants, following in the footsteps of William Penn, started to arrive in this country in the early 1700s. In the next fifty years they had learned the ways of the new land, and the guns they made go with their new way of life.

The good German gunsmiths who came over from the old country realized that the German Scheutzen were too big and heavy to be useful here. There was no need for the big, bone-crushing slugs that could knock down an elk or an aurochs. Also, the frontiersman who carried all of his worldly possessions on his back did not need the heavy bag of lead bullets that the large-caliber rifle required. Right after the 1750s, a new kind of gun made its appearance in Pennsylvania and in Virginia and perhaps elsewhere in the seaboard colonies. It combined the best features of the German Scheutzen rifle, with all of its accuracy, and the more delicate, graceful and much lighter English fowling piece. The advantage of this new gun, now called the Kentucky rifle, was that it was light. The smaller bullets were light, making it less of a chore to carry and using less valuable lead to keep it shooting. These guns were more often than not rifled, and that, combined with their long barrels, made them extremely accurate.

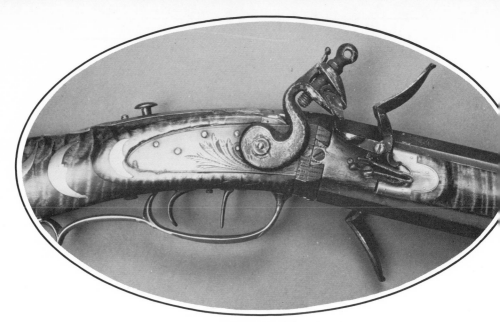

Swivel-breech (double-barrel) Kentucky rifle by P. Smith. This rifle, No. 250 in the Joe Kindig Collection, has thirty-three decorative silver and brass inlays, one engraved with an American eagle. The side plate has a rare engraving of a ship and the lock plate is engraved. The arm is early Federal period.

A whole generation of riflemen grew up on the westward frontier. When we went to war with England in the Revolution, these wild and woolly sons of the soil, who never saw a uniform and didn't know how to salute, massacred the best of the British troops at the battle of King's Mountain in South Carolina. With the Kentucky rifle, grew up a legend of the invincibility of the American soldier. The Kentucky riflemen, who, with the artillery, prevented the occupation of New Orleans by the British in the War of 1812, had a music-hall song written about them. One of the verses of the old song is the source of the name "Kentucky rifle," a gun made in Pennsylvania or Maryland or Virginia and carried, but never made, in Kentucky.

But Jackson he was wide awake and wasn't scar'd at trifles

For well he knew what aim we take, with our
KENTUCKY RIFLES

So he led us down to Cypress Swamp, the ground
was low and mucky,

There stood John Bull in martial pomp but here
was old Kentucky.

There were not enough homemade Kentuckys to go around when we went to war with the British. Besides, Kentucky rifles had their military limitations. They would shoot farther and more accurately than the British Brown Bess, but they took a lot longer to load. A trained British soldier was supposed to be able to get off seven shots a minute. As a matter of fact, he was pretty darned good if he could get off from three to four shots, but this nevertheless enabled him to perform in the required battlefield order of the day. The system required him to fire a shot in the general direction of the enemy and then fall back to reload while the next line of regulars had its turn. By the time that the third line had fired, the first line was ready to shoot a second round. The alternate to this was a tight group in a close formation. Three lines of infantrymen performed together. One line stood up and fired, the second line knelt and fired and the third line shot prone. This required precision and training, otherwise one of their own boys was likely to get hurt. It also required easy-loading muskets which would accept roll-in balls and could be loaded fast.

The Kentucky rifle didn't work that way. It took a tight-fitting lead ball which had to be hammered down the barrel with three or four sharp blows until it rested on the powder charge. The accuracy of the rifle depended on the ball fitting tightly and taking on the grooves from the rifling of the barrel. Loading took time, as much as three or four times as long as the Brown Bess or the Charleville.

The Kentucky rifle had another disadvantage in battle; it was too delicate to mount a bayonet. A Kentucky equipped with a bayonet would either simply have broken the forestock, because the barrel took the shock, or it would have shattered the stock at the throat, always the weakest part of the rifle.

For the Continental armies to fight, they had to have guns. The Americans got them several ways. The first and simplest way was by taking the Brown Besses from the British. These were liberated from local forts and arsenals and brought out from attics by Colonial soldiers who had fought in the French and Indian Wars on the side of the British. Other British arms were taken when the British evacuated Boston and when Burgoyne surrendered at Saratoga.

The early Congresses, realizing the desperate need for weapons, set up specifications for their manufacture by local gunsmiths. Many muskets were ordered, but not as many were ever delivered. These are called Committee of Safety muskets from the specifications drawn by The Committees of Safety of the individual states. The muskets that were made were a varied lot, revealing much Yankee ingenuity. Along with homemade cherry- and apple-wood stocks and hand-cast parts, you find British, French and Belgian locks, Brown Bess butt plates and Charleville barrel bands and sling swivels. It was a good gun if it shot, and it didn't matter how crude it was or how ugly it looked.

The big demand was for muskets, the infantryman's weapon. Few pistols were made or carried by the Continental soldier. Hand-guns were almost exclusively carried by officers, marines and sailors. John Paul Jones, who was practically our one-man navy in those days, is pictured in early-nineteenth-century lithographs wearing a Scottish bonnet (he was a Scot) and carrying five loaded pistols in his belt and one in his hand. This would seem to be an excess of fire power except that with all six pistols Mr. Jones was not better off than if he had had one of Samuel Colt's yet-to-be-invented six-shot revolvers.

Committee of Safety muskets are hard to find and still harder to identify unless stamped "U.S." or U.STATES," but there are quite a few U.S. 1795 and 1808 muskets around. These were produced to a tighter set of specifications by a number of independent gunsmiths.

The major source of guns used by the Continental soldiers was France. France was at war with England and it was to her advantage to supply arms to anyone who would fight the British. Over 100,000 French muskets were lend-leased to the new nation out of the stores of obsolescent 1763 Charleville pattern weapons. The French guns were so prevalent that they became the standard and were used as the pattern for the American-made 1795s and 1808s.

In 1836 Colt brought out his first percussion revolvers. These pistols were purchased by individuals and by field officers for their men for use in the Mexican War in 1846–1847. Colt revolvers, along with Allens, Manhattans, Remingtons, Savages, Smith & Wessons, Starrs and Whitneys, were carried during the Civil War and were brought home by the soldiers after the war was over. Many of these horse pistols were to see use again when the Civil War veterans from both North and South went West in the '70s.

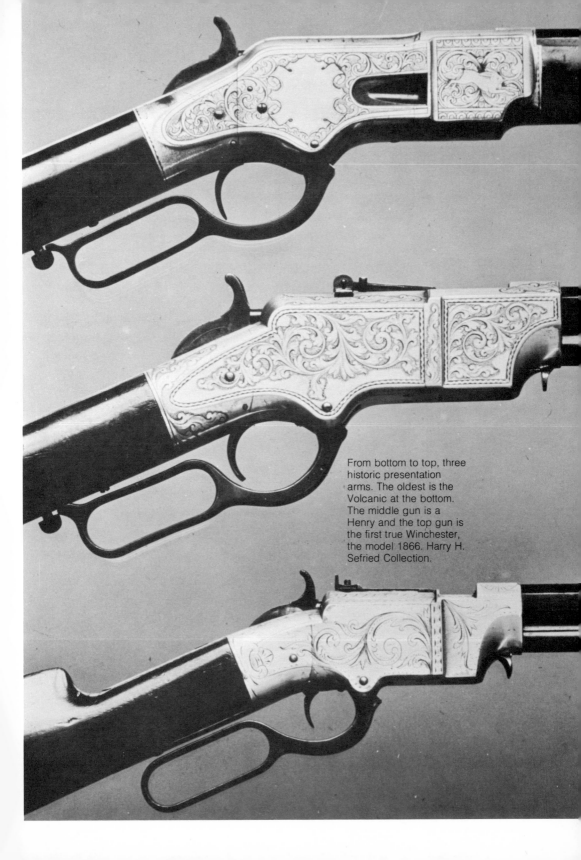

From bottom to top, three historic presentation arms. The oldest is the Volcanic at the bottom. The middle gun is a Henry and the top gun is the first true Winchester, the model 1866. Harry H. Sefried Collection.

Civil War guns and their makers are too numerous to list here, but the two guns that caught the public's attention were the Sharps rifle, for its accuracy, and the Spencer, because it was a dependable repeater. Winchester was building its "Yellow Boy," the brass-framed '66 repeater, but it was not considered to be heavy enough or to shoot a large enough bullet to be a military weapon. The Yellow Boy and Colt revolver were to win fame as "The gun that won the West" and the "Frontier." Contemporary cynics referred to the former as "The gun that made the West safe for the Army."

Civil War guns and western guns, especially the Sharps buffalo rifle, are eminently collectable and can still be found. Until a few years ago, collectors liked to shoot these old guns, but today they have become too valuable to risk the possible damage to springs and hammers.

The Kentucky rifle, which was in its prime from 1760 until about 1860, lost out to cartridge guns and mass production, but before becoming a collector's curiosity it had merged into the plains rifle. The plains rifle filled a practical need, as the Kentucky had in its day. The plains rifle was shorter, had a larger bore, and usually was made with a half stock. Most plains rifles, such as the Hawken, manufac-

The single-action Colt Army, also called the Frontier, This gun has a special hand-honed action and heavy carved ivory grips. It was presented by Colt to Andy Palmer, a trick shot in the 1920s and 1930s.

tured in St. Louis, were made for percussion caps. The flintlock period was almost over when the buffalo hunters worked their way across the Great Plains. The guns they carried had to be short, since they were saddle guns, and they had to be big bore for game such as buffalo, bear, elk and Rocky Mountain sheep.

Guns made up until the Spanish American War period (1898 to be specific) can be collected without a gun permit. After that date more and more cities and states have passed laws requiring permits for collectors if they have guns that will shoot modern cartridges. Before you start a collection of Colt automatics, Mauser or Luger pistols, it is a good idea to find out whether you will be in violation of the law and liable to have your collection confiscated by the police. In any event, do not collect machine guns. They are illegal everywhere unless completely disarmed and made unshootable. A federal permit to own an operable machine gun costs $1,000 a year.

For the beginning collector, the thing to collect is what is handiest and what you like the most. Guns made in the United States are an obvious starting point. In the next chapter you will learn the names of some of the more famous makers of American guns.

Who Made Guns In The United States?

FROM SMITH TO FACTORY

There was a time when every town in the United States had its own gunsmith and every little village and hamlet in Pennsylvania had a family or school of gunsmiths. Today you can count the number of factories making guns on your fingers: Colt, Harrington and Richardson, High Standard, Iver Johnson, Marlin, Remington, Ruger, Savage, Smith & Wesson, Stevens and Winchester. How many have I forgotten? In 1963 Colonel Robert E. Gardner published a directory called *Small Arms Makers*. There are 218 pages of American gunmakers with about thirty listings per page. That makes about 6,500 gunmakers over the past couple of hundred years. A handful of these men are worth noting along with examples of their work.

In the beginning of the colonization of North America very few guns were built from scratch. Settlers brought their guns with them from Europe, and if they were lucky they kept them in good condition. If the guns were broken there was a fifty-fifty chance that the local blacksmith could repair a spring or make a new cock to replace one with a fractured neck. Some of the earliest work on guns done in this country was in restocking with American fruit wood pieces made in England or the European continent. Thus, some of our earliest "American" weapons are only American by virtue of their wood.

Among the first gunsmiths whose names we know and whose work has survived are John COOKSON (1701 - 1762) and John PIM (*circa* 1722), both of Boston. Both men advertised repeaters which they may have made or had imported. Cookson, whose father was a London gunsmith, put his name on several single-shot muskets and on a Berselli-type of loose-powder repeater which is in the Nunnamacker Collection in the Fine Art Museum in Milwaukee. Pim's name appears on a snaphaunce revolving pistol which came to the Winchester Gun Museum in New Haven from the Ed Pugsley collection. There is some doubt about the authenticity of this marking, although the piece itself is genuine.

From town records we know the names of men who were employed to clean, repair, maintain and replace municipal stands of weapons in the towns of New Haven, New York, Philadelphia, Baltimore and Charleston, but we have not discovered many examples of their work. The mid-eighteenth-century American gunmakers whose names we do know make only a short list. It is worth calling them out here in case you have the good fortune to discover a firearm made by one of them.

Andreas ALBRACHT came from Germany to work in Lancaster, Pennsylvania in 1750, and a John ALBRECHT worked in Northampton County, Pennsylvania, *circa* 1745. One may have been the ancestor of Jacob and Henry ALBRIGHT, who were famous Kentucky makers at the end of the century. Edward and Thomas ANNELEY, gunsmiths, worked in New York in 1748 and in Philadelphia later. A musket has Edward's name and a pistol has "E. and T. Anneley."*

Edmund BEMIS was working in Boston in 1746. Samuel, John, Caleb and Robert BAKER could have been the first Lancaster gunsmiths in 1719. We know there was a Patrick BALLENTINE listed as a gunsmith in Charlestown, South Carolina, in 1720, and a John Valentine BECK who opened a gun shop near Winston-Salem in 1764. Enoch BOLTON worked in Charlestown in 1665, and Richard BROOKS in

*In the Joe Kindig, Jr. collection and the Donald Andreasen collection.

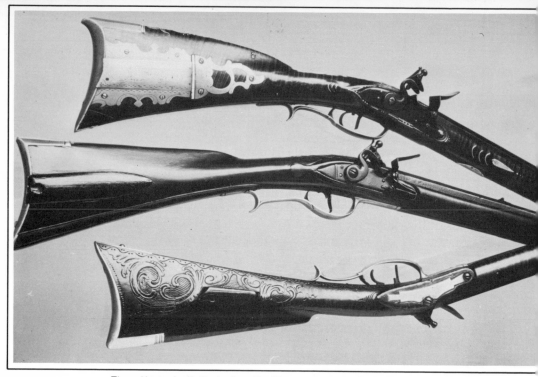

Three Kentucky flintlocks from the Harmon Leonard Collection. The middle gun is the oldest. It is pre-revolutionary, smooth bore, has a wooden patch box and a plain cherry wood stock. The right gun was made by John Bonewitz in the 1780s and is decorated with relief carved "C" scrolls. The left gun is signed "J. Alb" for Joseph Albright and was made circa 1800. It has the unusual feature of silver wire stock inlay. The piece is rifled .45 calibre with seven deep grooves.

Boston in 1675. John BRUSH came to Williamsburg from England with Governor Spottswood in 1718. Thomas BUTLER worked in Lancaster in 1749.

James CHAMBERS worked in Lancaster in 1750. Hermon DAVIES worked in Boston around 1650. Jacob DECHARD is supposed to have worked in Philadelphia in 1732, and Jacob DUBBS in Bucks County between 1735 and 1775.

Gideon FAUCHERAUD, Charlestown, 1708. William FOULKES in Pennsylvania, *circa* 1738.

Hermon GARRET was a gunsmith in Boston in 1667; James GEDDY, in Williamsburg in 1737; John GERRISH, Boston, 1709, and Richard GREGORY, same town in 1727.

John HAWKINS, John JONES and Robert FENWICK worked in Charlestown in 1699. John HENRY, the first of the famous Henrys, in Lancaster in 1747. Medad and Benoni HILLS worked in Goshen, Connecticut, in the 1750s and later with Thomas NASH of New Haven.

John HINDS, gunsmith, Boston 1745, Jacob HOOFMAN, Lancaster, 1750.

Benedict IMHOFF and Peter ISH were working in Lancaster in the '50s.

Peter KIEFFER landed from the first boat in Jamestown in 1608. Ephraim KEMPTON worked in Salem and Boston around 1677.

Mather LLEWELYN was in Lancaster in 1732, and Richard LEADER in Boston in 1646.

Duncan MACKENZIE, Philadelphia, 1731; Richard MANNING, Ipswich, Massachusetts, 1749; Philip MASSEY, Charlestown, 1730; George MATHIEWSON, Rhode Island, 1750; Thomas MATSON, Boston, 1658 - 1682; Samuel MILLER, Boston, 1742.

Ebenezer NUTTING, Falmouth, Maine, 1725 - 1745.

Hugh ORR, Bridgewater, Massachusetts, 1748; John ORTON, Philadelphia, 1725.

James PHIPS, Kenneback River, 1663.

Frederick RAUBER, Berks County, Pennsylvania, 1730s; Thomas RICKS, Boston, 1677.

John SCOTT, Charlestown, 1740; Nathaniel SHERMAN, Boston, 1692. Jeremiah SLITERMAN was the armorer to, and made muskets for, the colony of Georgia in 1766. A gunsmith by the name of SOLEIL was working in New Amsterdam in 1656.

Benjamin THOMAS worked in Hingham, Massachusetts, in the 1740s and '50s. Alexander TOULSON of St. Mary's was the first gunsmith of record in Maryland in 1663.

A gunsmith with the last name of VANDERPOEL worked in Albany in the 1750s.

Alexander WALDREN and William WALDREN, who would seem to be brothers, and Richard WATERS were working in Salem, Massachusetts, in 1632.

More digging in the archives of some of the older towns of the original colonies would surely double this list. These names come from Van Rensselaer, Henry Kauffmann in his book *Early American Gunsmiths*, and most recent researches by Donald Andreasen and Samuel Dyke.

By the 1760s we begin to find signed and dated Kentucky rifles. The earliest of these is a privately owned rifle made in Reading, Pennsylvania. It is signed and dated on the barrel "John Schreit

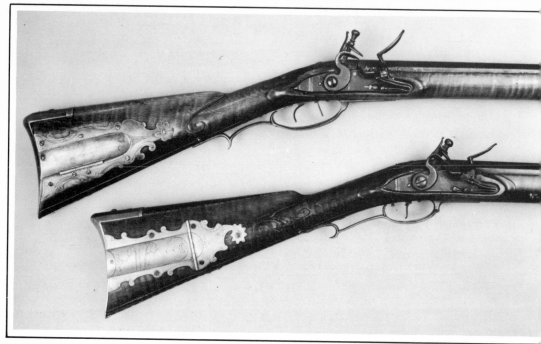

Two flintlock Kentucky rifles from Lancaster, Pennsylvania. Both guns exhibit the daisy-headed patch-box finial which was often used by later Lancaster makers. The top piece was made by Jacob Dickert, whose guns were the standard for accuracy in the Revolutionary War. The lower rifle is signed on the barrel "J. Ferree" Both a Jacob and a Joel Ferree worked in Lancaster in the late eighteenth century.

1761." The names and dates of the best-known Kentucky rifle makers can be found in Dillin's book *The Kentucky Rifle*, Kauffman's book, *The Pennsylvania-Kentucky Rifle*, Joe Kindig, Jr.'s *Thoughts on the Kentucky Rifle in its Golden Age*, in 561 pages, and my own little four-color picture book published in 1972, *The Kentucky Rifle*. All of these books list not only makers and their working dates but also show examples of their work.

When the American Revolution started, over a hundred gunsmiths were given contracts by the various state Committees of Safety. Surviving are muskets made by less than half of them, and it is a safe assumption that few delivered their quota. Some of them delivered nothing. We do have examples of the work of Thomas AUSTIN and BEEMAN of the Boston area; Jacob DICKERT and Joel FERREE of Lancaster; Samuel HALL of East Haddam, Connecticut; Eliphalet LEONARD, of Easton, Massachusetts; James HUNTER at the famous Rappahannock Forge; Abijah THOMPSON of Woburn, Massachusetts; Henry VOIGHT of

Philadelphia; Medad HILL of Goshen, Connecticut; A. VERNER of Bucks County, Pennsylvania, and Benjamin TOWN of Philadelphia.

The government arsenal at Springfield, Massachusetts, delivered its first musket to the U.S. Army in 1799. Eli Whitney received a government order in 1798 but hadn't delivered a piece until after 1801. Neither Harpers Ferry—or the Virginia manufactury delivered weapons until after 1800.

The chief concern of Congress in specifying the model 1795 musket was that it be plainly marked "U.S." and be stamped with an eagle to designate government property and discourage the soldiers from taking them home. There was a reason for this. Of all of the muskets from the Revolution, Brown Besses, Committee of Safety muskets and the 100,000 Charleville pieces, only 31,015 remained in government arsenals when an inventory was made at Washington's recommendation in 1793.

By the time Congress had undertaken to raise, arm and equip a federal militia in 1808, a considerable arms industry had sprung up. More than twenty independent makers and a number of substantial manufacturers were able to supply 85,200 flintlock muskets in three and a half years. While only a dedicated 1808 collector will recognize the names of many of the smaller contractors, the general American collector will have heard of J. HENRY, now of Philadelphia, Henry DERINGER, Simeon NORTH, Lemuel POMEROY, Nathan STARR, Asa WATERS and Eli WHITNEY.

Not only were military arms being produced in quantity but some fine custom gunsmithing was being done in the seaboard cities. A cased pair of gold and silver inlaid flintlock pistols in the Renwick collection are signed on the barrels and locks: "Haslett-Baltimore." They are as good as the best English pistols of the period. They were made by Major James HASLETT, a veteran of the War of 1812, who also contracted to make stands of muskets for the state of Virginia.

In the Smithsonian Institution are magnificent gold inlaid and engraved presentation pistols signed by Simeon North of Middletown, Connecticut. They were made to the order of the state of Connecticut for presentation to the naval hero MAC DONOUGH. They are engraved with a scene of the battle of Lake Champlain and have heavily chiseled, crisp gold plated furniture, including ramrod thim-

Pair of flintlock pistols signed "Haslett Baltimore." These guns, decorated with both gold and silver, were made around 1820 by Major James Haslett, who fought in the army in the War of 1812. The pistols were in the collection of William Renwick of Tucson, Arizona.

bles, trigger guard and butt plate. The barrels are bright with two gold lines inlaid. North took the order for the pistols with the understanding that they were to be made in his new factory, which was producing military contract arms. He succeeded in making these two deluxe arms by hiring two London gunsmiths to work for him. They were the ASTONS, father and son, who stayed and continued to work in Middletown, where they produced single-shot percussion pistols for the U.S. Army and Navy. John SWITZER, Lancaster, Pennsylvania, 1770–1780; Tobias GRUBB, Northampton, Pennsylvania, 1813–1820; HAMAKER in Philadelphia, circa 1810; and Peter WHITE, who worked in Uniontown in 1825, all produced fine silver-mounted flintlock Kentucky pistols in pairs.

In the 1810s and 1820s American inventive genius began to assert itself. John H. HALL from North Yarmouth, Maine, went to work at the Harpers Ferry Arsenal, where he was the superintendant for a number of years. He not only straw-bossed the construction of innumerable stands of conventional muskets but he also invented and produced the Hall breech loader for which the government paid him a royalty. The tip-up, breech-loading rifle was originally made in flint. These are quite rare today. Many more were made in percussion, up until 1844. In all, Hall received royalties for 22,872 rifles. His arm was used in the Florida Seminole War campaign in 1818 and in the Mexican War.

Another inventor, Joseph C. CHAMBERS of Washington County, Pennsylvania, was obsessed by the idea of multiple-firing weapons. One of his inventions, a superimposed ten-shot, sliding-lock, flint-lock rifle was made for him at the North factory in Middletown. He got an order for 200 from the U.S. Navy. He also invented a 228-shot revolver-shaped swivel gun with eight barrels which fired superimposed loads. It had a single flintlock lock. When you fired the gun it kept on shooting like a Roman candle for a good five minutes. Like all superimposed load guns, it was very dangerous to the shooter. The navy must have found this out because they only ordered ten of them and never reordered. As far as I know, none of these swivel guns survive in the United States. I found one of them in the attic of the Musée d'Armes in Liège, Belgium, but nobody could tell me how it got there. There is also a beautifully finished half-size inventor's model in the Rijksmuseum in Amsterdam. This one seems to have been submitted by the inventor, Chambers, to the Dutch Admiralty in

Collier flintlock revolver with primer magazine. Collier was an American inventor who had these revolvers made for him in London in the 1820s. This gun belonged to Colonel Colt and is now in the Wadsworth Atheneum Collection, Hartford, Connecticut.

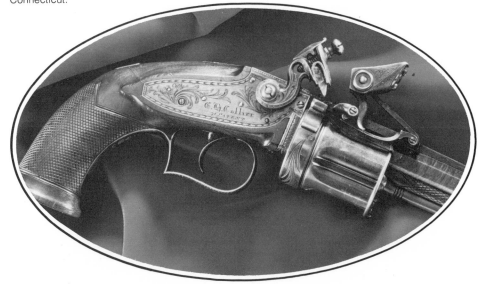

the hopes of getting an order. When the Admiralty no longer had any use or interest in the model, they didn't know what to do with it so they gave it to the art museum.

Three Americans, Elisha COLLIER, Cornelius COOLIDGE and Artemas WHEELER, invented and promoted a flintlock revolver. The pistol was first patented in 1818. Wheeler held the patent in the United States, Collier had a patent issued to him the same year in England, and Coolidge took the invention to France where he got a patent in 1819 and licensed it to be manufactured by LePage, who built pistols employing both tube-lock and percussion ignition. The English guns seem to have been made by London gunsmiths Evans and Rigby. Probably no more than four or five hundred revolvers were made in all and except for the patent model none of the U.S. manufacture seems to survive. The patents included a device for rotating the cylinder mechanically, but the early Wheeler model was hand-rotated, and so were some of the later models. The Collier also employed a primer magazine which was attached to the steel or frizzen. The guns were beautifully made and preceded the Colt revolver by eighteen years, but two things kept the Collier from being a success: it was conceived and invented in flint at the very end of the flintlock period, and it was a delicate and complicated piece of machinery apt to get out of order from the shock and recoil of actual shooting. Collector Clay Bedford, who has the finest collection of Colliers in the United States, or anywhere, has noted that while the flintlock Colliers are apt to be in new and crisp condition, since they were never fired very much, the percussion Colliers show heavy signs of use and wear.

Joshua SHAW, an Englishman, came to Philadelphia in 1817. He claimed to have invented the percussion cap in England in 1816 but he did not take out a U.S. patent for his invention until 1822. By that time a number of British gunsmiths claimed to have invented the percussion cap. London gunsmith Durs Egg put labels in his cased sets of pistols which stated "Inventor of the percussion cap." In any event, Shaw was the inventor as far as the U.S. Patent Office was concerned and his invention took off like a house afire. Within ten years no gunsmith in America was building flintlock guns with the exception of the U.S. Army, which continued to build flintlock muskets at the Springfield Armory until 1842.

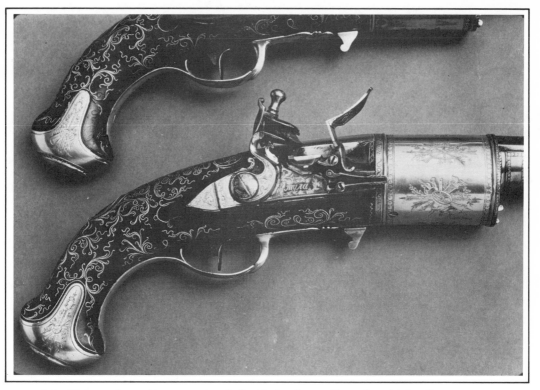

Pair of Tula revolvers with engraved and gilt cylinder sleeves. These fine pistols with their silver wire inlaid Circassian walnut stocks were made for a Russian prince by gunsmith Kalesnikov in about 1785. They are now in the Russell Aitken Collection.

Samuel COLT was one of the first to take advantage of the percussion system. He realized that the percussion cap made a revolving arm practical because it eliminated loose priming powders and allowed preloading six charges. Revolvers were nothing new and Colt never claimed to have invented them. He couldn't since wheel-lock and snaphaunce revolvers still exist which were made as far back as 1590. Even the Russians, who may not have invented baseball, had a fine flintlock revolver made by a gunsmith by the name of Kalesnikov in Kiev in the 1780s. What Colt envisioned and was able to patent was a revolver using caps that contained five or six loaded charges. The caps and a barrier between the nipples prevented fire from running from one charge to another, and the mechanism Colt had invented had a rachet, or finger, that rotated the cylinder mechanically, causing each hole in the cylinder containing a single charge to index perfectly behind the breech of the gun barrel.

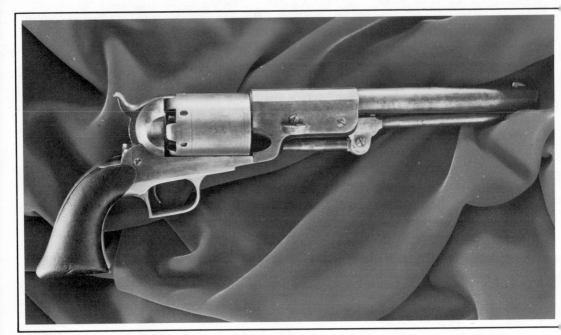

Colt Walker-model percussion revolver. This pistol was presented by Samuel Colt to Captain Samuel H. Walker and was shipped to him in Mexico in July of 1847. After Walker was killed in October of the same year the pistol was returned to Colt by a Captain McDonald. Wadsworth Atheneum, Collection, Hartford, Connecticut.

Practical as Colt's invention was, it took one bankruptcy, a fire, and a tremendous effort and great showmanship on Colt's part to get his idea off the ground. His first Paterson, New Jersey, plant went broke. The small production of Paterson Colts makes them very valuable to collectors. The next Colts were made for him under contract by Eli Whitney. These, too, were produced in only limited quantity, so that a Whitney Colt is also rare and expensive. Finally, Colt built his own factory in Hartford, Connecticut, where he made a financial success due in part to orders that he received for military pistols and carbines for the Mexican and the Civil wars. Even then, Colonel Samuel Colt's problems were not ended. In the beginning of the Civil War his Hartford factory burned to the ground and he had to start from scratch to rebuild. Colt died in 1862, after having established an arms empire that survives today.

Colt's greatest asset was his showmanship. As a young man he demonstrated laughing gas and underwater mines to make money to pay for the design work on his revolver. When he began to manufacture he became a master at giving the right people gifts at the right moment. His gifts were always Colt revolvers and they were finished to reflect the interest and the importance of the recipient. This has proved to be a bonanza for the collector because there are many rare and beautiful engraved and gold and silver inlaid Colt revolvers that were made and presented to generals, presidents and kings. The czar of Russia and his brothers, the crown princes, all received magnificent cased Dragoon and Navy Colts which are still like new in the Hermitage Museum in Leningrad. Other one-of-a-kind presentation pieces were made by Colt and engraved by Gus Young and presented to the sultan of Turkey, the king of Sweden and American army officers too numerous to mention.

One of the finest presentation sets to come from the Colt factory was made for the Colt Works Manager E. K. Root when he retired. An example of every firearm then made by Colt, long-arm and revolver, was finished as elegantly as possible, inlaid, engraved, stocked in elaborately carved wood from the Charter oak tree in Hartford and framed in mirrored glass cases that are almost as ornate as the guns themselves. The gift must have overwhelmed Root, who moved out to the Middle West on his retirement. Anyway, some of the presentation set stayed in Hartford and can be seen in the Museum Collection at the Connecticut State Library, while other parts of the set are in the Mellon collection in Pittsburgh.

While Samuel Colt was the glamour boy of U.S. revolvers, and his guns bring the highest prices, revolver collectors recognize that Colt was not alone—or even the first. Between the time that patents were issued to Collier and Wheeler for their flintlock revolver in 1818 and the first Colt patent for his percussion revolver in 1836, there were other revolver patents issued and revolving guns made. Henry ROGERS of Middletown, Ohio, got a patent for a four-barrel percussion revolver in May 1829. In the following month, June 11, 1829, J. and J. MILLER of Rochester were granted a patent and proceeded to manufacture a finely finished seven-shot pill-lock revolving rifle. James Miller, John Miller, William BILLINGHURST and C.A. BROWN in New York state all produced first-rate revolving rifles during Colt's early years. James B. Smith of Newington, Connecticut, who knows more about revolvers than any collector I know, lists twenty-two early revolver manufacturers including Benjamin BIGELOW who built fine guns in Marysville, California, before the Civil War.

The nineteenth century saw the United States take the lead in both gun design and manufacture. American inventions were largely in the area of repeating mechanisms, but the machinery to produce guns was of equal importance. ROBBINS and LAWRENCE of Windsor, Vermont, were basically toolmakers who happened to get involved with gun manufacture. Originally three partners, Samuel Robbins, Nicanor Kendall and Richard Lawrence, they started with a government contract to build 10,000 percussion rifles for the army. They completed the contract on schedule and went on to build the prototype of the Winchester, the Jennings tubular-magazine rifle. Being practical men, they realized that the inventor of the safety pin, Jennings, had come up with a very weak gun mechanism and a hopeless "Rocket Ball" cartridge which was nothing more than a lead bullet with a little primer mix in the base as a propellent. They managed to get the specifications changed on the Jennings and finished a contract for a couple of thousand guns by making them in single shot. Both Daniel WESSON and B. Tyler HENRY, who were to have an important part in the evolution of the first Winchester, worked for Robbins and Lawrence. In 1852 Lawrence left the firm to set up the first Hartford factory to produce the famous SHARPS rifles, but by this time Robbins and Lawrence were so well known in arms-making circles that the British sent over ordnance specialists to look at Robbins and Lawrence's machine tools. They took back with them tools and ideas that revolutionized the British military arms industry.

Winchesters, Marlins, Colts and Smith & Wessons all have their army of collectors, and a number of books have been written for the collector about the production of each company. I have seven books on Winchesters alone in my library and eight books on Colts. One or more books have been written on each of the following gun makers: BALLARD, BROWNING, DERINGER, GATLING, MANHATTATAN, NORTH, PARKER, REMINGTON, SHARPS, STEVENS, SMITH & WESSON and WHITNEY. These, plus more than a hundred general books on American arms, will provide the interested collector with all the basic information he needs to place alongside of actual examination of arms themselves. There are many collectors of Kentucky rifles, New England guns, Civil War guns, Confederate weapons, plains rifles and martial arms—enough for each group of collectors to have their own clubs and sometimes their own publications. In all, there are probably over two hundred thousand arms collectors in the United States. What can they all collect? That is the subject of the next chapter.

What To Collect

THERE ARE STILL PLENTY LEFT

With several hundred thousand collectors and an ever-growing interest in antiques of all kinds, what is left to collect? The answer is *plenty*. If you have the time and money there is no end to what you can collect. If you don't have the money, you can substitute knowledge. Skill and judgment in recognizing a rare piece can really stretch a poor collector's dollar. With luck, a good memory and concentration, a poor collector can become a rich collector.

Bill Locke of Cincinnati built one of the great all-time collections of American firearms and especially cased presentation Colt revolvers. Bill was neither rich nor poor, but he had a tremendous memory and follow-through. Bill never forgot a gun, a price, who owned it, and who had owned it before that. When he found a piece he wanted, he kept after it until he owned it. It might take years, but some day the owner would weaken from sheer exhaustion, and Bill would carry home the prize.

Bill knew all about the arms he collected. He had seen them all and he remembered every detail of every arm he ever examined. When he found a piece that he wanted, he was always willing to pay for it, but often the owner would not want to sell. At that point Bill would find out what the collector wanted more than money. Usually it was another gun. Bill would put as much effort into collecting a piece to trade as he would in adding a piece to his permanent collection.

Some years ago I happened to mention to Bill that I had seen the Chambers piece in the Rijksmuseum in Amsterdam and also a pair of silver-mounted Hall breech-loading flintlock pistols in another European museum. Bill wanted both these pieces in the worst way. He already owned two pairs of Hall breech loaders and this pair would corner the market. The Chambers inventor's model was one of a kind. Bill knew there was no chance that either European museum would be permitted to sell him pieces from their collection, but he also realized that neither of these weapons meant very much to the museums they were in. They were American pieces and did not relate to the history or the tradition of the rest of the museum collections. Bill then went to the head of each museum and asked if they would trade their American pieces for older pieces made in their own country, for example, Dutch snaphaunces of the sixteenth century for the Chambers swivel gun. Bill got immediate interest.

Then, with his well-known persistence, he set out to pry Dutch snaphaunces from one of two American collectors who owned several fine ones. The collector wasn't impressed. He liked his own snaphaunces and he didn't care to exchange them for money. The collector told me the story. He got so that he was afraid to go to his office because every Monday morning, like clock work, the phone would ring and Bill's cheery voice would be on the other end of the wire with a better offer.

This story does not have a happy ending. Bill died before he got these particular pistols, but had he lived, the Chambers and the Hall pistols would have found a home in Cincinnati just as sure as shooting.

The guns I have been talking about are pretty rich for the average collector, but Bill did not always aim for such fancy guns. What he did all his life will be a good guide for any starting collector. He was brought up in Nebraska, where he attended every farm sale and auction he heard of. When a neighbor collector had to sell his collection Bill scrounged around, raised $200 and bought the lot. He didn't want all the guns in the collection, but this investment gave

Breech-loading pistol made by H. Smith in Norwich, the invention of Smith and Percival. This oddball pistol was formerly in the U.S. Cartridge Company collection and then was owned by Bill Locke in Cincinnati, Ohio.

Cased Colt dragoon pistols with smooth ivory grips and fine scroll engraving by Gustave Young, in the Bill Locke Collection.

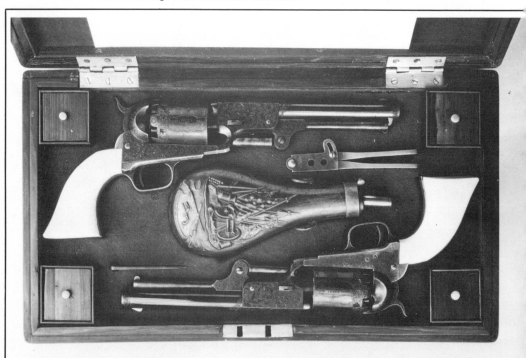

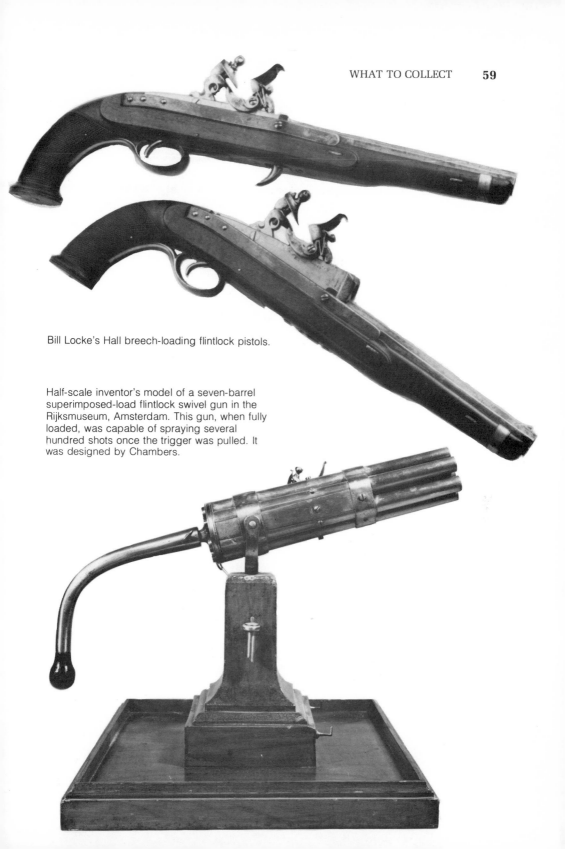

Bill Locke's Hall breech-loading flintlock pistols.

Half-scale inventor's model of a seven-barrel
superimposed-load flintlock swivel gun in the
Rijksmuseum, Amsterdam. This gun, when fully
loaded, was capable of spraying several
hundred shots once the trigger was pulled. It
was designed by Chambers.

him a trading stock. He traded off the guns he didn't want for guns that fit his own collection. Horse pistols and carbines were the most common guns where Bill came from, along with souvenirs of the Civil, Spanish American and First World wars. Fine guns were a rarity because, as Bill said, "In my part of the country, when an old gun wore out we threw it in the hog pen and that was the end of it. In New England when a gun was old-fashioned or no longer of service it was stored up in the attic in case it should ever be of use. The result was, of course, that there were a lot more antique guns in New England than in other parts of the country."

When Bill got married, he used to take a vacation with his wife, driving through New England looking for auctions and stopping at antique shops. The dealers got to know Bill and would save guns to show him when he came through their towns each summer.

Some of the guns Bill collected are hard to find or very expensive today. In order to be of as much help as possible, I will list some of the categories I run into at antique stores, gun shops and gun shows.

The oldest guns you are apt to find in your searches are flintlock military muskets. The run-of-the-mill musket is likely to be pretty well beat up after having been around for two hundred years or so. The wood may have chips and gouges out of the stock, and the barrel and lock are more than likely to be covered with rust. As often as not, the original flintlock will have been replaced during the working life of the gun with a percussion hammer. The steel and its spring will have been removed and a tube tapped and threaded into the barrel where the touch hole was. Into this tube will be screwed a nipple to hold the priming cap for the percussion system. You can recognize whether or not the gun was originally made as a flintlock both by the general shape of the arm and also by careful examination of the lock plate. Look at the front of the lock plate. If you can see the screw holes in the plate where the frizzen spring and bridle used to be, you can be sure the gun was made in flint.

Since you are not apt to find a very old gun in mint or new condition, it may pay you to buy a basket case and restore it yourself. If you do decide to work on the gun yourself or have the work done by a gunsmith, the question is, How far should I restore the old piece? Too little restoration leaves you with an eyesore and too much restoration may destroy part of the original finish and the value of the piece as an antique arm. One of the biggest problems is whether to reconvert the piece to original flintlock. There are two definite schools of thought on this. The subject is good for an argument whenever two antique gun collectors get together. The whole matter of restoration and gun care will be covered in some helpful detail in Chapter 10. Even if you don't intend to do the work yourself, it will help to understand what has to be done.

The first step after buying any old gun is to clean it. Gentleness and moderation are the words. You can always take more off, but you can't put old finish back on. Once the metal and wood have been cleaned, your chances are much improved for finding makers' marks, proof marks, dates, the name of the place where the arm was made and military markings. All this information will add to the value of your gun and to the pleasure you will get out of knowing its history.

Everything I have said about military muskets also applies to Kentuckys. Kentuckys are most apt to have been converted to percussion from flintlock since they were hard-working guns and the owners did not lightly discard them. Lots of Kentuckys were also made in the percussion period. If the stock is flat and sort of board-shaped instead of having deep contour and perhaps some stock carving, there is a possibility the gun was made late enough in the nineteenth century to have had a percussion lock originally. It is silly to convert to flint a gun that never was a flintlock to begin with.

When you get past the period of handmade guns and come to the machine production of pistols, revolvers, and rifles, the condition and finish of the arms becomes very important in determining value. Guns made by machinery must be either in very good condition or be rare because only a few of a particular model were made. Ideally, as a collector, you want both qualities. Don't buy junk; and, most important, check for matching serial numbers of the parts. But if you limit yourself to perfect specimens, it may be a long time between finding additions to your collection.

Martial arms are around in some quantity and at prices a beginning arms collector can afford. This is especially so as one gets beyond the flintlock period and the few short-production-run experimental guns, such as the two-shot Lindsay pistol, of which only a few hundred were made. Some martial arms collectors want arms from all periods of American history. Others tend to specialize in arms of a particular period or war. Books listed in the selective bibliography deal with the arms of each war in which the United States was engaged. And then there is Gluckman's general book on martial arms, *Identifying Old U.S. Muskets, Rifles and Carbines.*

Collectors who start out being interested in everything often wind up collecting the arms of one particular manufacturer. This is why there are so many special books on a single manufacturer and his guns. Other collectors will pick a type of arm. It may be single-shot rifles. There are four books on this subject by the same author. It may be revolvers, target guns, hunting weapons, air rifles, double-barreled guns, magazine repeaters or underwater pistols.

Since every type of gun has its group of aficionados, how do you pick what you want to collect? There are examples in public collections of every type of gun to be collected. Some are rarer than others, but once you have settled on what interests you most, you will find ones you can afford even if you have to scrimp and save in order to own them. The important thing is to decide what you want most to collect. This is not as difficult as you might imagine.

Most of us come to gun collecting by one of only a few routes. As young boys, we have been fascinated by the legends of the West and young America, both intertwined with gunsmoke, heroism and action. As we get a little older we may get a chance to do some target shooting or we are taken hunting by our parents. Naturally, after shooting someone else's gun you want to own your own. This is the end of the interest in guns for 99 out of 100 shooters. There are over 22 million licensed hunters and only 200,000 collectors. If a guy is interested in arms only to the extent of wanting to own a good shotgun for hunting in the fall, or in owning a target-sighted High Standard for use on a police pistol range, he is not a dyed-in-the-wool collector. I would not even include the all-around hunter who owns a working gun for every type of game but couldn't care less for a handsome piece of another era. He may collect trophies and have an interest in keeping the finish of his hunting guns, but his guns are tools, pure and simple. They are not art, antiques or history-evoking, and when he gets too old to shoot bear, he has no more use for a high-powered rifle he once took to Alaska.

You must examine the motives that started you collecting. Most of us start because we are ga-ga about guns. Obviously we can't know everything as beginners. Nicely furnished guns are more attractive than bum ones, and we learn to tell the difference between a good and an indifferent polish and blue job on the metal. The wood of modern guns is either plain or checkered, and we soon become knowledgeable about the quality and the fineness of the checkering and the grain and finish of the walnut stock or grips. From there our collecting bent can go in a dozen directions. Some will want to concentrate on fine modern weapons. To them, the precision and finish of the piece is all that counts. They may be interested in the more decorative pieces with examples of engraving and gold inlay work by some of the top living engravers such as Alvin White in this country or René Delcour in Liège. Both men, and a handful of others, here, in England, Belgium and in Ferlach, Austria, can engrave and inlay animals, hunting scenes, emblems, patriotic motifs or even, if you wish to supply the art, they will create a custom decoration for your favorite piece. This might be a portrait of your favorite horse or a naked babe doing handstands.

Some collectors are skilled at mechanics and may even have some training in engineering. Obviously, their interest in a firearm will lie in the mechanism. Unusual loading and ejection systems for the magazine repeater will fascinate this collector more than the most graceful engraving or stock carving. An example is my friend Harry Sefried, one of the best gun designers in the business. Harry is an engineer, a designer of mechanisms and an inventor. He is naturally interested in what makes the darned thing go, whether it is a racing car, a motorcycle, a crossbow with a hair trigger, or a magazine repeater of the nineteenth century. Harry has a Cunningham and a pile of car parts in his garage and one of the best collections of Winchesters, Remingtons, Whitneys and Marlins you ever laid eyes on. What is more, Harry can take apart every one of his guns and show you at what stage of development the particular model had reached. Harry is interested in fine workmanship and creative design. He couldn't care less if the particular gun he owns belonged to the king of Spain or Pancho Villa. (One of his guns did belong to the latter.)

Another kind of gun-collecting cat is really collecting history. This collector can look at a beat-up New England Colonial fowler or

Pancho Villa's ivory-stocked Smith & Wesson.

musket, but instead of seeing its worn and rusted remains, he can envision the Pilgrim father defending from an Indian attack, his block house on the edge of the wilderness. The flintlock musket with regimental numbers is not just one of 2 million military arms made in England for the wars with France, it is the very weapon that the brave Captain Pitcairn carried to his death at the battle of Breeds Hill. Sometimes these historical collectors do uncover some pretty exciting stories from the markings that they find and can interpret on antique arms—and sometimes their wishful thinking gets in the way of the facts. A plain and undistinguished military piece becomes blown out of all proportion because of a false assumption that the arm belonged to General Washington or President Kennedy. I once delighted a man and made a friend for life by giving him a 50-caliber lead pistol ball that had belonged to Napoleon. The ball was genuine; it really had come from a cased pair of pistols which had Napoleon's name on them. Without a shadow of a doubt the pistols and the ball had belonged to that great man. Nevertheless the round lead bullet was still a round lead bullet exactly like any one of millions of other round lead bullets cast in the same manner. I'm glad my friend has the pistol ball, because he is something of a Napoleon nut.

Still another type of collector is only interested in the decoration and design of the arms. Often this collector will have had some training or exposure to art and can see in a fine arm the school or discipline that caused the piece to be decorated in a certain way. A knowledge of art is a great help in tracing the history and value of an unknown or otherwise unmarked piece. Gun design is traditional if it is good, and definite rules are always observed in the choice of decoration of arms. A knowledge of the reason for, and the source of, a design cut in steel or carved in the stock of an antique weapon can tell you not only what country, but what city and at what time a particular gun was built. Often, even more precisely, the design and workmanship of a piece will lead you to the school or the very person who made the gun. This is as true of an Italian snaphaunce as of a Kentucky rifle.

Special knowledge and interest will often dictate the direction a collection will take. A friend of mine collects double rifles, and so he should. He knows better than the men who still make them how to regulate them so that the bullets fired from both barrels find the same

American long fowler with Belgian lock signed "Jacques Valée à Liége." The gun belonged to Colonel Ezra Taylor, who built Fort Halifax in 1754.

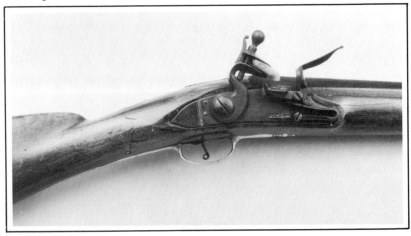

Modern big-game rifle in .375 calibre made by Wesley Richards in Birmingham, England. The sidelocks are fully scroll engraved and the stock is finely checkered. The illustration shows the gun apart with telescope mounted on the barrels and the watch-case-engraved hand detachable locks.

point of impact at a given distance. This is an art, and many brand-new guns from the factory do not target as they should at forty or a hundred yards, depending on whether the double is a rifle or a shotgun. George Rowbottom can take a double, new or old, and with what is to me a kind of black magic, figure out what combination of what kind of powder and what shape of a bullet of what weight will give the gun its perfect performance. This is his whole interest in life, or, at least, in collecting. Once he has unlocked the secret of a new double gun, he has no further interest in that particular piece. Somewhere he has noted the correct load for the double on a scrap of paper in case he ever needs to shoot that particular gun again. After that the gun goes on the gun rack, along with a hundred or more of the finest double rifles and shotguns in the world.

Many beginning gun collectors start by collecting modern or recent weapons. Sometimes their collecting interest is aroused by a single fine piece which comes their way or by a gun which belonged to some member of the family—a trapdoor Springfield that belonged to Grandfather or a Colt service 45 automatic that Dad carried in the First World War. In many cases the beginning collector is all over the place. He is apt to call himself a general collector and be a sucker for anything bright and shiny. Little by little, as he learns more about the pieces in his collection, he finds that some are of more interest than others and begins to specialize in the collection of that particular type of weapon.

Some collectors never do find themselves. Collector Harold Berger of Collegeville, Pennsylvania, started as an armor collector. He owned a big Victorian house with high ceilings and ample floor space. When he started collecting there was still quite a bit of armor to be had. Harold filled the house with suits, half suits, shields and helmets. Every place you turned, you found yourself face to face with old ironsides. As you climbed the stairs you had to share the landings with a knight in armor. One fine day Harold got fed up with all of this sheet metal and put it up for sale. He got a good price for the armor and put the proceeds right back in another collection. This time he went in the opposite direction, which may in part have been dictated by his building a new house with lower ceilings and not so much waste space. Harold then collected miniatures. These included antique miniature wheel locks and crossbows, right up to half-scale Winchesters and Colts. A good part of Harold Berger's collection is illustrated in my book *Miniature Arms*, published in 1970 by Winchester Press and McGraw-Hill. Shortly after my book appeared, Berger lost all interest in miniatures, sold his collection, lock, stock and miniature barrel to Walter Clode of Westley Richards in Birmingham, England, and took up collecting antique watches and automata. Harold is consistent about only one thing: He is a collector.

Clay Bedford is a very important antique arms buff in the San Francisco area. When Clay became interested in guns, he sought the advice of Colonel Arcadi Gluckman. Together they visited the well-known arms dealers here and abroad and attended the gun auctions in London and Lucerne, Switzerland. Gluckman is an expert on U.S.

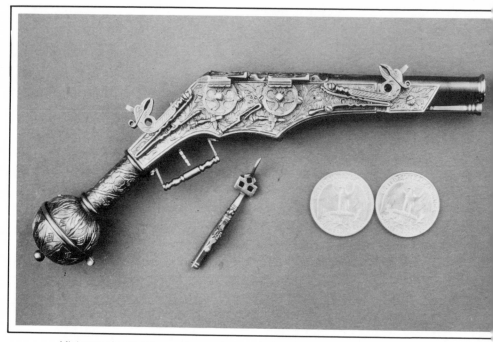

Miniature of a double-wheel, superimposed wheel-lock all-metal ball-butt Nuremberg pistol of the late 1500s. The scale of the miniature is indicated by the twenty-five-cent pieces in the photo.

martial arms and has written the definitive book on the subject. An old army man, Gluckman even prefers his martial arms to be army-associated and not navy. Clay tells the story that the colonel tried to talk him out of bidding for a Colt revolver because it was a navy model.

After a year of association with Gluckman, Clay Bedford's gun room was beginning to fill up with U.S. martials and an occasional Kentucky, and Clay was finding that firearms collecting wasn't all that much fun. One fine day Clay discovered what he really liked to collect and he has been going hell-bent-for-leather ever since. Long before Clay took up gun collecting he had had a serious interest, with his wife, in antique English silver. Whatever Clay undertakes, he does thoroughly and well. Clay studied and memorized the makers and their marks, the hallmarks of the different British sterling silver producing centers and the system of date stamping by letter which tells you the exact year a piece of English silver was made. With this background, Clay was a natural to collect silver-mounted English guns and pistols, and that is just what he did. With a world of enthusiasm, knowledge and stick-too-itiveness, in just ten years Clay was able to put together such a comprehensive collection of British and Irish firearms that the Metropolitan Museum of Art in New York asked to exhibit them in a special loan show and published a 192-page catalogue illustrating the pieces.

So what is around to collect? The answer still is that there are plenty of guns of all kinds to suit the taste of any collector. It is true that certain American arms such as presentation Colts and Winchesters have gone skyhigh in price. This has had a desirable effect on collecting in general. Twenty years ago the members of the American Society of Arms Collectors were predominately Colt and Winchester collectors with a smattering of U.S. martial specialists. Today this same group covers a much wider variety of collecting interests, from wheel-lock guns and crossbows to powder flasks, cane guns, combination weapons and miniatures. You may ask, "Where should I look for the kind of guns that I want to collect?" and "Where will I find the best collections of guns for study?" I'll answer these questions in the next chapter.

Where To Look

SHOWS, SHOPS, AND LUCK

Choice antique guns turn up in the damndest places. A nearly mint H. Aston percussion pistol was hanging over the fireplace of a shore cottage rented by a friend of mine. My friend had no interest in firearms, and the man who owned the cottage had no idea where the pistol came from and suggested that I take it home with me. I did, and after cleaning off a light, even coating of rust which had not pitted the soft steel surface, I had a fine martial pistol. If I hadn't been a fool and traded it off, my Middletown Aston would be worth over $500 today.

One of the best cased pairs of LePage percussion pistols belonged to a no-nonsense engineering friend of mine who was a great and enthusiastic hunter. He came to me one day and offered to buy a good Churchill shotgun I then owned. I said, "No, I bought the gun second-hand because it fitted me very well and I couldn't afford to go out and have a custom-fitted shotgun made to my measurements." Realizing that he couldn't get the Churchill from me for money, he came up with the offer of the LePage pistols. I told him he was crazy to think of selling or trading the pistols, as they had been in his family since they were purchased new in LePage's shop in Paris over a century ago.

This conversation meant nothing to my friend who, I have said, was intensely practical. He said that he didn't give a damn about the family pistols. He couldn't shoot them. What he needed was a working shotgun to shoot pheasant. That is what he got and I have a pair of ebony-stocked, case-hardened and gold inlaid LePage pistols in mint condition with extra hammers, extra nipples and a full set of tools including a key to raise and lower the rear sight.

I must admit that these are two examples where I was lucky. I won't bring up examples where I came out second best, but that is all in the game of collecting. If you won all the time, it wouldn't be any fun.

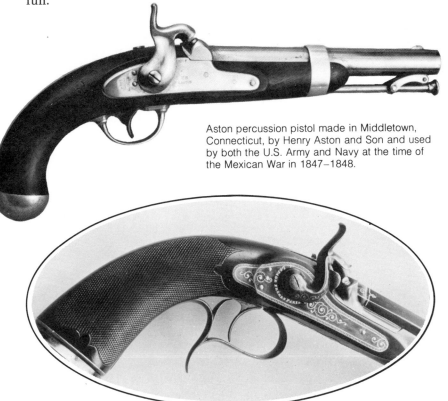

Aston percussion pistol made in Middletown, Connecticut, by Henry Aston and Son and used by both the U.S. Army and Navy at the time of the Mexican War in 1847–1848.

Elegant and simple LePage pistol which belonged to the same family for 100 years. There is a pair of ebony-stocked percussion pistols with simple gold scroll inlays in the blued steel. The pistols are in a fitted case with all of the original tools and spare parts — just as they were when they left LePage's shop before 1854.

You cannot expect to find all the good guns you want to collect hanging over somebody's fireplace. You must develop a system of knowing where to look. The biggest marketplace for guns of all descriptions are the gun shows, big and little, which go on all the time all over the United States. Not a month goes by that doesn't offer at least one gun show in your neighborhood. This completely American institution will range in size from a quiet trading session at the local antique gun club to the Anaheim, Disney Land, Las Vegas, Ohio, Baltimore or Hartford gun shows where exhibitors come from all over the country and hundreds of display tables will be covered with guns and accouterments for sale or trade.

These shows are great schools for the beginning collector as well as for the more advanced specialist. By looking and asking questions, a lot can be learned without having to shell out hard cash.

Most all of the larger shows have, in addition to guns for sale, educational exhibits by private collectors and by arms manufacturers. The show sponsors encourage these non-commercial exhibits by offering handsome prizes in several categories for the best presented or the most informative exhibit.

Next to gun shows, which are increasing in number and quality all the time, there are established dealers who are antique or modern firearms specialists. Sometimes you will find a good selection of arms in your local hardware store. This is more apt to be true if you live in the country. In the larger towns and cities there are specialized new and antique gun dealers like Red Jackson in Dallas, who deals mostly in antique guns, or Kerr's Sporting Goods Store in Hollywood, where fine new weapons predominate.

The big cities, with their stringent gun laws, haven't discouraged crime on the street, but they have driven legitimate antiques arms dealers either up the wall or out of town. Abercrombie and Fitch still has an antiques department, but a look of pain crosses the salesman's face every time you say, "I'll buy it." The paper work required by the Sullivan Law in New York City for the purchase of an antique gun that hasn't been, and couldn't be, used in the commission of a crime is staggering. This burden of useless paper work grew to be too much for Bob Abels, the dean of antique arms dealers in the East. Bob closed his store at Sixty-fourth Street and Lexington Avenue in New York and moved up to his farm across the river from West Point, where he has his store and sees collectors who call him in advance. He is not too far from other important arms dealers in the Northeast, including Norman Flayderman, Herb Glass, Alan Kelly, John Malloy, Glode Requa and Eric Vaule. All of them are located in the country north of New York City in either New York State or across the border in nearby Connecticut, and all of them are worth a trip, with a call in advance, if you can arrange to be in the neighborhood.

Whether you are a joiner or a loner it will help you to be a better collector if you join your local arms collectors club. It will also help you to find treasures which may be right under your nose. If you are a member of a collectors club, the other members will get to know what you are most interested in and will pass along information when they hear of a gun they think you would like. Members also like to trade back and forth, which is a good idea. One is less apt to get exaggerated ideas of what a piece is worth. Also, pieces acquired this way do not carry a dealer's mark-up, which can double the price each time a gun changes hands.

There are approximately fifty collectors clubs in the United States affiliated with the National Rifle Association. They range in size from one with fifteen members to the huge Ohio State Association with over eight thousand. If you want the name of your local gun collectors club, write to the American Rifle Association headquarters, 1600 Rhode Island Avenue, Washington, D.C. 20036. New members are always welcome.

If you want to buy guns, many dealers put out periodic lists of arms for sale. These catalogs are offered through collectors magazines such as *Guns, Guns and Ammo, Gun World, The Gun Report, Shotgun News* and in more general magazines such as *The American Rifleman*.

If you want to study fine guns, there are two places where you can find them. The first is in private collections. Don't be shy. One of the main reasons collectors collect guns is to show them off to other collectors. Most of the guys I know are delighted to show their collections to serious amateurs and are happy to spend time explaining the features of their pieces. Arms can also be seen and studied in art and historical museums. The finest gun collections are to be found in the following museums. (Other exhibits come and go. Loan shows, such as the Clay Bedford show of English arms, are on exhibition for four or six months and then are broken up and replaced by other exhibits.) Here is a list of the museums with permanent collections and a brief note about each:

In Annapolis there is a small collection of arms at the *U.S. Naval Academy* including two swords which belonged to naval hero John Paul Jones.

The *Walters Art Gallery* in Baltimore has a fine collection of beautifully decorated European antique arms.

The *George F. Harding Museum* on East Randolph Street in Chicago houses one of the great collections of firearms and accessories, swords, polearms, cannon and Remington paintings and sculpture. In order to see the collection you have to be a serious collector and call the museum to make an appointment. It is not open to the public.

The *Cleveland Museum of Art* houses the Severance collection which includes suits of armor, helmets, swords, firearms and polearms.

The *Henry Ford Museum* in Dearborn, Michigan, has both American civilian and military firearms *and* a complete gunsmith's shop.

In Hartford, Connecticut, there are two public collections of arms, both heavy on Colts. The *Wadsworth Atheneum* has an armor hall and Colonel Colt's own personal collection, much of which is unfortunately not on exhibition. The *Connecticut State Library* in Hartford, adjacent to the Statehouse, is open to the public and exhibits the fine Colt Factory collection.

The *Los Angeles County Field Museum* houses a fine collection of all kinds of guns, arms and armor including a number of pieces from the Metropolitan Museum on permanent loan.

The *Milwaukee Public Museum* owns the Nunnemacher collection of firearms which is large enough to have a two-volume catalog. The present directors of the museum unfortunately have the collection hidden away in closets.

The *Winchester Gun Museum* in New Haven, Connecticut, has one of the finest gun collections in the United States. Its eight thousand firearms come from the Winchester Repeating Arms Company Ballistics Laboratory, where inventors brought their inventions in the nineteenth century so that Winchester could make ammunition for them, and the Edwin Pugsley Collection which Olin Chemical Company bought when they took over the Winchester Plant. It is open to the public including Saturday.

The *War Memorial Museum* of Virginia is located in *Newport News*. They have over four thousand exhibits including weapons from the Revolution, the War of 1812, the American Civil War, the Spanish American War and World Wars I and II.

The *New Windsor Cantonement* in New York State is a reconstruction of an American Revolutionary fort. It houses weapons and other military weapons.

The *Metropolitan Museum of Art in New York City* has the greatest arms collection in this country. Over 13,500 items of arms and armor are either on exhibition in the Great Armor Hall and in adjacent exhibit rooms or in the study collection which is available to students on request. The Metropolitan Museum of Art also houses a fine library on arms and armor. The European Arms and Armor Collection, incorporating the Riggs, Stuyvesant and Dean Collections, is one of the best and most catholic in the world. The Oriental arms collection, especially the Japanese collection, also presented by Bashford Dean, is unique.

The *United States Marine Corps Museum* at Quantico, Virginia, exhibits the firearms and edged weapons used in amphibious warfare since the establishment of the Marine Corps in Colonial times.

The *National Park Service Museums* are scattered all over the eastern part of the country. They include, going from north to south, the following collections:

The *Springfield Armory Museum* in Massachusetts with one of the most complete collections of modern military small arms.

The *Morristown, New Jersey, Historical Park*, "Washington's Headquarters," owns a small but important collection of arms including Washington's inaugural sword, an agate-handled hunting sword of Washington's, the only surviving military Ferguson breech-loading rifle, a fine French and Indian War Coehorn foot mortar.

The *Fort McHenry National Monument* in Baltimore has the E.

Berkeley Bowie collection of American Military and Confederate firearms.

There are three National Park Service collections in Virginia, including the *Fredericksburg National Military Park*, containing good Civil War firearms; the *Petersburg National Military Park*, with Civil War weapons, especially artillery equipment; *Colonial National Historical Park* at Yorktown with excavated seventeenth-century arms from Jamestown and battlefield relics from the British surrender at Yorktown in 1781.

Fort Frederica National Monument at St. Simons Island, Georgia, contains archaeological recoveries documenting the type of arms used by the British in the 1740s.

Fort Caroline National Memorial in Jacksonville, Florida, has a small collection of arms and armor of the mid-sixteenth century.

The *City Art Museum of St. Louis* has a selective collection of arms and armor chosen as works of art.

The *Fort Ticonderoga Museum*, New York State, contains an extensive collection of swords, firearms, American polearms, paintings and military paraphernalia of the Revolutionary War period.

The *Smithsonian Institution's National Museum of History and Technology*, Washington, D.C., has housed an extensive collection of arms, military uniforms and equipment. In addition, hundreds of pieces from the William Renwick Firearms Collection will be on exhibition after 1975.

The *West Point Museum* at the United States Military Academy is open to the public. Its exhibits include excellent dioramas of historic battles as well as a fine collection of weapons arranged in chronological order. The study collection covers military firearms of all periods.

Colonial Williamsburg in Virginia has some arms and armor in the reconstructed buildings, but is especially noteworthy for its gunmaker's shop, where Kentucky rifles are made from scratch, by hand.

Back on the trail of guns to buy, some guns are to be found in antique shops, but not as many as there used to be. One of the reasons for this is that the study of arms is a specialized pursuit and the average antiques or junk shop proprietor doesn't have the interest or ability to learn about arms and cannot tell one gun from another. If he

buys a gun in a lot of household furniture, he is most apt to take it to a
gun dealer rather than price it too high or too low. The gun dealers
and the hobby shop proprietors, therefore, wind up with most of the
finds, and that is where to look, unless you follow estate sales and
auctions.

Country newspapers such as New England's *Newtown Bee* and
Shoreline Times (second section) are full of information about antiques and old houses for sale, including notices of private sales and
auctions. Sometimes the auctioneer will provide a breakdown in his
ad, listing swords, guns, and other items.

A final source for fine arms are the antique art auction houses.
Because of the firearms laws, there are no longer any auctions of
firearms at Parke Bernet or other art auction houses in New York City,
but the British firm of Sotheby, who owns Parke Bernet in New York,
have showrooms in Los Angeles and run periodic sales of fine American arms. In London, the two great auction houses, Sotheby and
Christie, each run monthly arms sales. Some of the finest arms in the
world change hands there and in the sales rooms of the Fischer
Gallery in Lucerne, Switzerland. The highest price ever paid for a
gun, $305,000, brought a Louis XIII flintlock from the Renwick Col-
lection in Tucson via Sotheby back to the Metropolitan Museum in
New York.

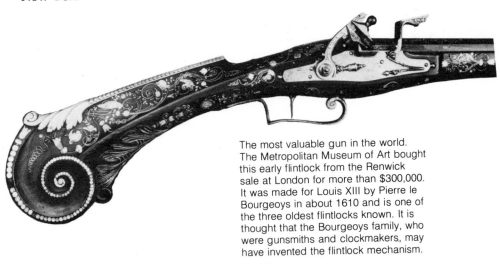

The most valuable gun in the world.
The Metropolitan Museum of Art bought
this early flintlock from the Renwick
sale at London for more than $300,000.
It was made for Louis XIII by Pierre le
Bourgeoys in about 1610 and is one of
the three oldest flintlocks known. It is
thought that the Bourgeoys family, who
were gunsmiths and clockmakers, may
have invented the flintlock mechanism.

Civil War sharpshooter posing in a studio with his Billinghurst Rifle.

If you have a chance to attend a Sotheby or Christie auction, it will be an education, but don't expect to come home with a prize unless you bring plenty of money. European collectors are paying higher prices for every type of arm than are American collectors, and that goes for even purely American-made arms. A check of recent European prices shows similar guns bringing two to two and a half times as much in European galleries and shops as they do from American dealer and gun shows. This has put an end to the importation of fine European antique arms by rich American collectors. Now, when an important American collector such as William Renwick dies, his collection, if not left to a museum, is most often shipped to the auction houses in England or on the Continent because the pieces will bring much higher prices there than they would if sold here. There are no more rich Americans but there do seem to be many rich German, Japanese and Swiss collectors.

Good guns are constantly turning up, which is what makes gun collecting such an exciting hobby. Just as you have concluded that you have explored every possible source for firearms in your neck of the woods, some old lady will teeter out with a mint Civil War Billinghurst sharpshooter's rifle complete with telescope. It will have been lying high and dry under the leaves of an old house since it was put there wrapped in greasy flannel rags over a hundred years ago.

Did this ever happen to me? No! But I can dream about it, and it has happened to collectors luckier than I. Perhaps you will be the one.

And how about the little old lady who found the beautiful gun in the attic, with documents to prove its genuineness, who turns out to be pushing a fake. This happens, too. It is important to know how to tell a fake from the genuine article. With gun values going up every day, there is a very tempting field for the arms faker. Chapter 7 will tell you how to avoid some of the pitfalls.

How To Tell A Fake

A TRICKY PIECE OF BUSINESS

Fakes come in all shapes and sizes. Few firearms are built from the start as complete phonies. In almost all cases fakes are created by changing or modifying or improving an existing arm. Unlike forgeries of painting or sculpture, the faking of a complete firearm is an enormously complicated matter requiring all sorts of skills and all kinds of specialized machines. Special dies would have to be made for even the lowliest job of stamping assemblers' marks, and at each stage of faking, the chance increases of a minor error giving away the whole structure.

A creditable Rembrandt or a Renoir can be faked if the art faker is talented and studies not only the master's style but takes pains to use the same materials, pigments, canvas, wood, varnish and fatigues the finished work to the correct degree. To fake a gun from scratch, requires a complete machine shop plus the assistance of skilled specialists to carve or checker a stock, mill out a frame, make and temper springs, drill, ream, rifle and polish a barrel. Finally, a fake gun has to be finished like the antique original, which means that after polishing, marking, decorating or engraving and stamping with specially prepared dies, the steel must be colored in the same way that the antique was blued or case-hardened. This requires special furnaces if the bluing is to be done with bone or fish oils. Even supposing all of these things were possible, a minute dimensional error in making a small part or the style of lettering used in the stamping dies can betray the arm as a fake.

Much more common than a fake from scratch is the "improvement" of firearms and armor. This kind of fakery was practiced more than a hundred years ago. Collectors still remember the name of Samuel Pratt, a well-known London arms dealer back in 1854. Sam had lots of customers for elegant gilt and decorated wheel-lock pistols and hunting arms of every description. His supply of these fine weapons never seemed to cease. The more extravagant the requirements, the greater effort was put forth by Sam's skilled workmen. They made no effort to manufacture these arms from bar stock. They bought plain military weapons from old European arsenals whose stores had become obsolete. These weapons were perfectly authentic. They were as old as they were supposed to be, and even today's sophisticated tests of the wood and metal would have shown them to be antiques. Also, the pieces bore the hard-to-fake stamps of the Nuremberg or Brescian barrel makers, stamped in the metal while still hot. All Sam Pratt did was to take perfectly good plain weapons, worth little or nothing in those days, and engrave, etch, inlay and fire gild the exteriors. If a wheel-lock ball-butt was plain, skilled furniture inlay and veneer specialists were hired to inlay bits of bone, ivory and mother-of-pearl. The workmanship of the craftsmen was remarkably good. It was so good that Pratt's masterpieces wound up in the collections of the rich, the famous and the most discriminating. Dr. Samuel Rush Meyerick, who organized the arms collection in the Tower of London for the king of England, bought pieces from Pratt for his own private collection. So did Napoleon III, King of France, and his arms expert, the Count of Nieuwerkerke. Many of Pratt's fakes were acquired by Parisian art dealer Frederic Spitzer, who was not above employing Paris jewelers to add a semiprecious stone here or there.

Sir Richard Wallace, an English collector, bought the Nieuwer-

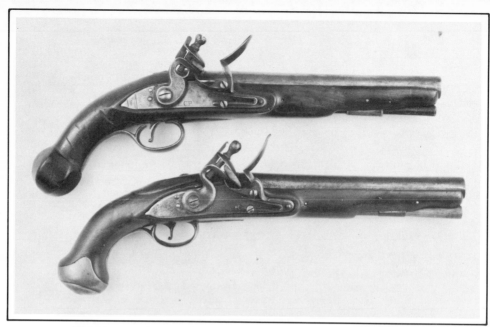

Rappahannock Forge flintlock pistols — real or fake? Many years ago it was known that the Rappahannock Forge had produced firearms during the Revolutionary War, but no surviving arms were known. Then two pairs of pistols surfaced. They went from hand to hand, one pair winding up in the collection of the Winchester Gun Museum, the other in the William Locke Collection. After these pistols had made their appearance, others turned up that were quite different in appearance. Bill Locke swore that his pair was real; but Tom Hall, curator of the Winchester Gun Museum, is equally positive that both pairs are clumsy fakes. This is the pair that belonged to Bill Locke.

North and Cheney flintlock pistols. These are real Middletown pistols produced in 1797, and not the French Model 1777 with fake stamps. William Locke Collection.

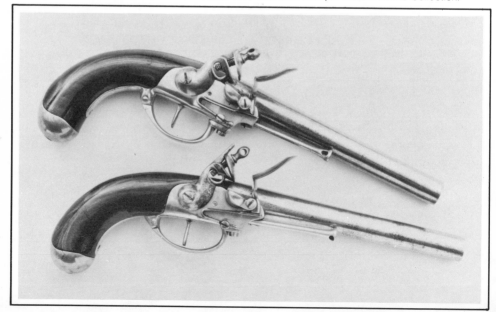

kerke collection when France lost the Franco-Prussian War in 1871. He also bought the Meyerick collection from Spitzer after having missed an opportunity to buy it when it was first offered for sale in England. The cataloguer of the Wallace collection, Sir James Mann, says that "Wallace did not himself possess a great knowledge of the subject" [arms], and later on, in his introduction, Mann points out that "The distinguished provenances of his acquisitions ensured their being of the first order . . . ." Some of them were.

It is a lot easier to recognize the weapons Sam Pratt improved today than it was a hundred years ago. The designs and decorations that Sam's workmen inflicted upon honest but plain arms were accepted by contemporary eyes accustomed to those designs. Today some of the "enriched" decorations stands out like a sore thumb because they now shine forth as what they are—Victorian decor applied to Charles I or Louis XIII period pieces.

Another common faker's trick is to take a garden variety firearm and with judicious minor changes in the markings make it into a much more valuable and rare piece. A classic example of this is the transformation of the Charleville flintlock pistol, brought to this country by the French at the time of the Revolution, into an infinitely rarer North and Cheney pistol made in Middletown in 1797. This was not hard to do because the North and Cheney was copied as exactly as possible from the French model 1777 pistol. The arms faker had to grind or mill off from the barrel and lock plate the markings of the French arsenal and replace them with the "North and Cheney" signature. Most collectors would not notice the difference, especially if the arms faker took the trouble to copy an authentic North and Cheney stamp. In this way, a French pistol worth a few hundred dollars was transformed into an American pistol worth thousands.

If you are ever offered a rare piece like this for a very low price, get the opinion of all of the experts you can. In the case of the North and Cheney, an expert noticed that the flat sides of the breech of the barrel were unequal in width, indicating either very poor gunsmithing or that (as was the case) the gun had been tampered with and one side had been ground down, making that face wider than the others. Unfortunately, the expert did not make his discovery until after the collector had been taken.

Certain types of accidents, in addition to normal wear and tear, bring down the value of an antique arm. Some cleaning and restoration is permissible. A missing screw can be replaced if one is careful to find or make a screw with the same pitch, the same number of threads, and the same head shape and size. If the screw were hand-made on the original gun, the replacement had better be handmade or it will look out of place. Finish is the first thing to be lost on old weapons. Here it is better to clean a piece and leave it bright or with some residual bluing than it is to polish off all of the remaining finish and reblue the gun with cold chemical blues which are sold at most gun shops. In the first place, polishing an old gun can destroy its value unless done by an expert. If the sharp lines of the original piece become blurred or rounded by holding the piece too long or in the wrong direction on the buffing wheel, the value of the piece drops far below what the same piece would be worth with a spot or two of rust or pitting left alone. If you suspect an arm has been reblued, hold the arm so that the straight flat surfaces are toward the light. If you see any bellying or irregularity, suspect the piece. Also if the edges are not sharp and crisp, the polish job which preceded the bluing may not have been done at the factory. If there is pitting from rust under the polish and blue, run like hell.

The things to look for which may have been replaced or worked over on the older guns, such as wheel locks and flintlocks, are the cocks themselves. These are apt to crystallize and shatter from use. Often the arm will be found to have been welded, brazed or replaced. Springs break. A broken spring inside a wheel or flintlock doesn't improve its value, nor does a weak spring which may be an improper replacement. An unfinished piece may be the result of the restorer's being in a hurry or not having finished the spring properly before tempering it. Always take off the lock plate of an old gun. It will show you whether work has been done on the mechanism. It will also tell you if the stock is a replacement. Often a new stock will have been fitted to old metal parts, the old wood having rotted away or been eaten by worms. The new stock may have a fine glow of old walnut on the outside but have a telltale pallid look on the inner surfaces, which are covered up by the barrel, the lock or side plates, or the trigger guard or butt cap. Sometimes these areas have been stained an ap-

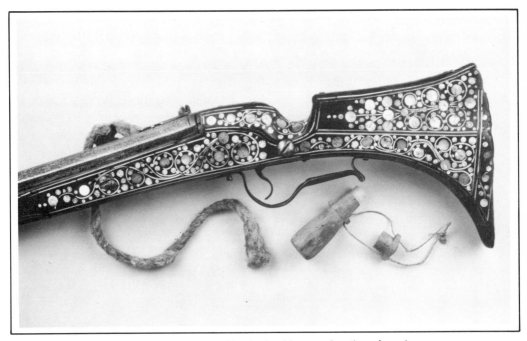

Big matchlock musket from the low countries. Hundreds of ivory and mother-of-pearl inlays have been replaced in the stock of this gun. No effort has been made to improve the gun, but much work has been done to conserve and restore the arm to its original condition. The van Zuylen Collection, Liége.

propriate color to make them appear aged. In this case one can often detect a slight odor of new stain or varnish. One Carlsbad wheel-lock pistol I was considering purchasing had a strong odor of shoe polish in the nicely browned lock cavity. Conversely there is a characteristic smell of old wood from a genuine piece. It is something like the slightly stuffy acrid smell that one gets in old attics, especially when they have been closed for a long time holding the summer heat.

Replacing missing inlays is considered legitimate by all but the purists. It is not, however, correct to engrave replaced ivory or mother-of-pearl or silver inlays unless a similar one, which is original, remains on the gun. Otherwise the etching or engraving one might do will be as phony as the improved guns of Samuel Pratt. It would be like adding the missing arms to the Venus di Milo without knowing what the original looked like.

There is usually very little finish on the metal parts of very old arms. Only those pieces which have remained in private collections and museums and have received constant care and not too rough cleaning will have survived with their original blue and fire gilt finishes. Unfortunately, there has persisted over a period of years a certain type of eager-beaver European arms dealer who cannot resist ruining any piece that falls into his grasp. A good piece may be suffering from nothing more than the normal neglect and need only a good cleaning with mild soap and water and a drying coat of fine oil and a hard-wax polish. Some European dealers are not content with saving what is left of the finish of an old, good piece; they want to make it shinier, and in the process they wreck it by grinding off every vestige of original finish and then polishing the entire surface of the arm right on top of old pits where there were deep pockets of rust.

The resulting gun is a mess. Everything that should have been smooth and sharp is slightly irregular and rounded. The finish is gone and so is the fit where wood meets metal. Where there should be at most a hairline or no crack at all the metal and sometimes the wood, too, will be rounded off like two pillows pushed together. Front sights, if there were any, get ground away to a nub. Gilding or light etching? Forget it. The wood gets a heavy dip of shellac and *voila!* you have a fine gun for a tourist. Fortunately, with painstaking care you can remove the shellac or old varnish from wood and sometimes from the metal parts as well, but the grinding and polishing can never be undone. Unless the piece is very rare and you despair of ever finding another like it, pass these guns by and look for better specimens.

A collector of the 1930s in the United States had a taste for this type of finishing of firearms. Unfortunately he had lots of money and could afford to purchase some fine weapons. Gus Diderrich liked his antique firearms bright and shiny. To his credit he did not have a botch job done on his pieces. The man or men who worked on his guns were master machinists. They did not turn the sharp edges or spoil the crispness of old arms, nor did they spoil the original fit between wood and metal. All that happened to Gus's guns was that he made new guns out of old ones. There was not a bit of the original gun left when Gus got through. His guns were finished so bright that they looked like the chromed radiator of a Rolls Royce. I have seen a number of Gus's guns in private collections, museums and up for sale on dealer tables. You can't miss one of them, they are so bright they stand up and hit you when you enter a room. Too bad, because Gus ruined a number of irreplaceable fine arms by destroying the original finish.

A lot can be learned about the history of an old arm by looking at the bottom of the barrel after removing it from the wooden stock or fore-end. If the gun has been tampered with or worked over, you may find holes inletted into the stock where there are no corresponding lugs to hold barrel pins. Conversely, you may find spots where barrel lugs have been filed off and nothing left except a smear of metal on the barrel to show where they were. Sometimes old lugs have been removed and new lugs soldered or brazed on to fit into a new stock for that barrel.

Locks are often replaced on guns, or old stocks are reworked to take locks which are replacements and never intended for the shape of the previous inletting. In these cases you will find a poor fit of the lock to the stock or little bits of wood added to fill up holes which were left between the old inletting and the new, differently shaped lock. Also, attention should be paid to the inletting itself. If wood has been cut away where it serves no purpose in housing a part of the present lock, it may be that the present lock is not original.

Stocks are perishable, often falling victim to worms, wood rot, fire, being dropped and broken, or being stored on wet, stone cellar floors. The number of spare parts thus created is amazing, and there

Small hand cannon of the Neuchatel type. The barrel dates from the fifteenth century. The stock is a reconstruction based on contemporary illustrations of Swiss infantry. Since no original wooden stocks survive from this early period, a properly identified reconstruction is not a fake.

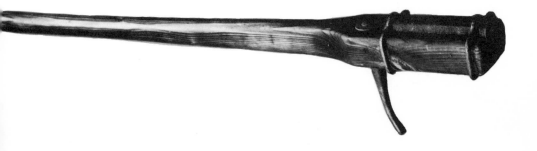

are endless gnomes in the Black Forest, the cantons of Switzerland, the foothills of the Italian Alps around Brescia and Gardone, in the industrial city of Birmingham and along antiques row in both Paris and Rome where sharp-eyed fixers work endlessly to match up credible combinations of locks, stocks, barrels and bits of furniture from here, there and everywhere. The best protection a piece can have is its provenance, but the provenance, too, can be tailor-made unless you buy the gun from an honest thief who gives you his word he just stole it from a museum. Protect yourself as best you can by minute examination of the wood and metal parts for any sign of adaptation or modification and for any new work done to make things fit which were not always together.

Another clue is the decoration. Does the engraving of the side plate match the design and workmanship of the lock, the trigger guard, the butt cap? Often there will be a telltale difference in quality between parts of the same gun. I have a snaphaunce pistol which is quite honest. That is, all the parts are genuine. There is only one thing wrong with it. The parts of the pistol came from several other pistols, none of which were quite a pair. The lock is magnificent. A beautifully carved sea serpent cut out of a block of steel holds the battery, and an equally handsome cock swings on an elegant carved steel lock plate. So far, the gun is of museum quality, but here we stop. All of the rest of the gun is nicely decorated with lightly etched design. It is a good workmanlike arm with a slight concession to decoration. The rest of the metal parts of the gun bear absolutely no relationship to the elegant lock. They come from two completely different arms which just happened to fit this particular pistol stock without any obvious modification.

Watch for a wide variation of quality of workmanship and degree of decoration on the same piece, which can indicate a composed weapon. There are, of course, understandable exceptions. For example, you might well find a crude repair made by an American blacksmith on a fine European hunting piece which the owner brought to this country in its early days of gunsmithing. Also watch for pairs of pistols made from one gun with the genuine parts divided between the two.

When the percussion cap was invented, everyone who wanted to keep and shoot old guns had them converted from flint by removing the frizzen and frizzen spring and drilling out the touch hole, inserting a tube to which a percussion nipple could be attached. The original cocks were replaced with percussion hammers mounted on the same axle. Hundreds of thousands of guns were converted in this fashion between 1820 and 1865. For the last forty-five years, gunsmiths have been busy reconverting old guns back to flint. Naturally, a gun which has been reconverted is not as valuable as the same model in original flint. The easiest way to tell whether the gun has been reconverted is to check the lock. If the lock is new the reconversion is obvious. Gunsmiths, however, try to keep a supply of lock plates with authentic old marking on them for just this purpose. Fortunately there is another way to check a suspected reconversion. When the gun was altered from flint to percussion, the touch hole was enlarged and usually threaded to receive the tube or drum for the percussion nipple. When the percussion attachment is removed for reconversion, a large hole is left in the breech of the barrel. The gunsmith making the reconversion has to plug this hole with a new piece of steel and then drill a new touch hole into the chamber. It is nearly impossible to disguise this new piece of metal which has been driven in, threaded or welded. It is true that some fine flintlocks had gold- or even platinum-lined touch holes to prevent the corrosion which occurs with the burning of the priming powders. It would easily be possible to use gold or platinum to fill the hole caused by reconversion if the pistol or gun were of sufficient quality so that the gold touch hole did not look silly. For instance, a gold-lined touch hole on a Brown Bess would be a dead giveaway because no one originally would have spent the time or money on a military weapon.

Finally, before we leave the subject of touch holes, check any old weapon you are thinking of purchasing to see if the touch hole lines up with the pan, and also see whether, when you lower the cock, a flint in the jaws is in the right position to strike the frizzen and push it forward. Guns are supposed to be working machines. If they don't line up so they can function, there is something rotten in Denmark.

In the good old days, when guns were much cheaper than now, some dealers tried to make their arms more salable by adding names of makers or of prominent owners on the locks or the escutcheon plates. These forgeries were usually engraved, which would have been correct for an owner's name, but suspect if it was supposed to be the maker's name, since a gunsmith would be much more apt to use a die to stamp his name or his mark. Years ago a dealer in the Boston area bought a copy of Van Rensselaer's book on American guns and handed it to his engraver. The result is a whole rack of New England muskets, rifles and fowlers in the Renwick collection. They are all perfectly good guns which would have sold today on their own merit, but now they have had gunmakers' names from van Rensselaer's book engraved on the locks or barrels, sometimes on top of old rust pitting.

Longtime American gun collector Howard Greene tells the story about a gun and hardware dealer in one of the little towns in New England's Housatonic Valley who proudly showed him his newest acquisition which he had in the front window of his store. It was supposed to be an inscribed, cased pair of flintlock presentation duellers. On the lid of the box, which had only recently become a case for pistols, was an important plate. On the plate was the legend, "From George Washington to his friend Benedict Arnold." The dealer proudly told Howard that he had paid a lady, who was descended from Benedict Arnold on the distaff side, $1,000 for the pair. The "pair" however were heavy Belgian flintlock horse pistols originally made up not in pairs but by the tens of thousands for use by the French cavalry. There were lots of these pistols and even more unassembled parts left over in the Liège arms factories around 1900. Sears and Roebuck bought thousands of them and advertised them in an early turn-of-the-century catalog as decorators at $1.75 apiece. Howard said that the hardware man really believed in his pistols and Howard had difficulty escaping before the roof fell in.

Everything I have said about the finishing and refinishing of old weapons applies equally to newer ones. A refinished Colt or Smith & Wesson, Remington, or Winchester loses value if it has been re-polished and reblued, even if the work was done at the factory, and sometimes because the work was done at the factory. Often, repair work is not a strong point of an arms manufacturer. I have had an automatic pistol refinished by one of the fine old Connecticut firms who had originally made it. They ruined the arm.

A final note of caution about any mass-produced weapons with interchangeable parts. Make sure that the numbers stamped on the parts all match. A Colt 1851 Navy-model percussion revolver will have a serial number of five or six digits. The number will be stamped in full on the gun, and each of its component parts will carry the last three digits. For example, if the full serial number of the Navy were 123,456, each individual part of the gun should be stamped with the last three numbers, 456. This is why the first thing a Colt collector will do when he is examining a new gun is to turn it over to see if the numbers on the frame, the trigger guard and the grip frame are the same.

These numbers can have been mixed in several ways. If the piece saw military service, parts from different guns can have been assembled incorrectly. If work was done at the factory, the numbers of new or replacement parts are supposed to match the original serial numbers, but at times, I suspect, mistakes were made. Finally, a gun-shop repairman may have used what parts he had on hand to make a functioning weapon. This would be especially true during the working life of the piece. Few owners who wanted to shoot their gun would care or even notice whether the serial numbers were consistent.

Now that you know some of the things to look for in a suspect gun, I want to point out the rosier side of gun collecting and tell you how to go about finding a rare gun and how to recognize it when you do find it. That is the subject of the next chapter.

How To Spot
A Rarity

IT'S ALL A MATTER OF KNOWING

The greatest asset any collector can have is knowledge. Knowledge of arms can be gained in two ways. The first and most useful is knowledge from having seen actual arms. The careful study of a gun is rewarding in a way that cannot be duplicated by looking at a picture or reading about it. On the other hand, it would be impossible for any one collector to see and handle every type of gun and every variation of that type. This is why there are more than a thousand books on firearms in print. They all help to round out and supplement what the collector has learned by actual observation.

A collector sees what he wants to see in a gun. One person will see and instantly recognize a mechanism. The function of the parts and the interaction of one part on another will be apparent to him. Another collector will be intensely aware of the decoration of an arm. This person will recognize the grade and quality of the decoration, whether the engraving is the work of a master or an apprentice, whether it is an original concept or a bad copy of someone else's work. Russell Aitken, who has the finest private collection of beautifully decorated arms in America, is one of the latter. He can tell more about

Flintlock wender made by the original LePage and dated 1767. It comes from the collection of Louis XV and is one of the few surviving royal French guns upon which Napoleon did not stamp his initial "N."

Pair of chiseled steel flintlock pistols signed "Acqua Fresca" and dated 1681. These superb pistols were in the Musée de l'Armée in Paris. One of the pair was stolen from the museum. Keep an eye out for it.

Rare smokestack gun in the Kunsthistorische Museum, Vienna. The smokestack was to keep the smoke of the primer powder flash from the royal hunter's eyes. The barrel is signed by one of Austria's most famous gunsmiths, Hans Faschang. The elaborate wood carving of an intricate maze of tiny animals entwined in the verdure of the forest is the work of a man whom we know only as "Der Meister der Tierkopfranken."

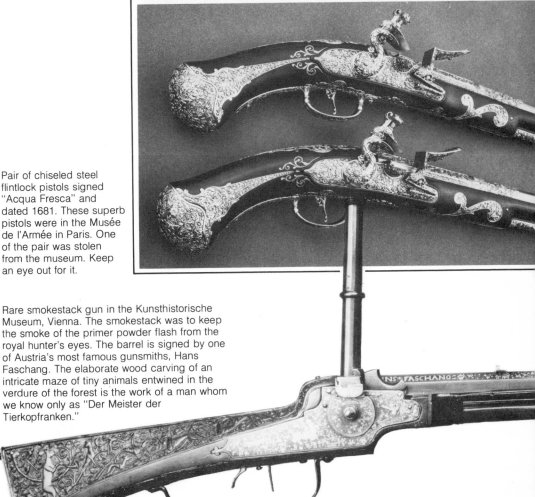

a fine gun without touching it than many a dealer. His interest, however, is almost exclusively in the beauty of the piece. If his armorer tells him that the mechanism is O.K. that is enough for Aitken. He would never be curious enough about the inside of a gun to remove the lock plate for study. This is understandable enough when you learn Aitken's background. He was trained in the arts at academies here and abroad and studied ceramic sculpture in Vienna.

Russell Aitken can spot a rare, finely decorated gun even if it is one in a collection of thousands. He learned about firearms by having seen good ones. The Kunsthistorisches Museum where he studied in Vienna houses one of the finest and oldest collections of arms and armor in the world. The collection, which was started by the emperors of Austria before 1600, was visited almost daily by Aitken when he was a student. His art training helped him to remember the details and fine workmanship of these royal pieces. Russ has also been a hunter and clay-pigeon shooter—he was one-time World Champion at skeet — and has had guns built to his specification even to the point of commissioning artists to make original drawings which he has then supplied to the gun engraver for inlaying in gold on the receivers of his fine shotguns. Today he lives within a stone's throw of the Metropolitan Museum of Art, and next to the curator of arms and armor Russ probably knows most about the decorated arms in the Met's collection.

Museums are certainly the best place to look for fine weapons. I have listed in Chapter 6 where the major museum collections are located. There are also many, many fine smaller collections in town and state historical society museums. There are loan shows to be looked for. For example, the best exhibition of Kentucky rifles, including the treasures from the individual members of the Kentucky Rifle Association, were exhibited at the fine little museum in York, Pennsylvania, owned and operated by the York County Historical Society. There will probably never be as fine a collection of Kentucky rifles on exhibition in one place as there were for six months in York. If you missed this show you will find the rifles illustrated in color in my book *The Kentucky Rifle*, but until you have actually seen and handled one of these fine guns you won't understand all its romance and mystique.

Gun shows are also excellent places to learn about different kinds of guns. Especially valuable are the educational exhibits which are put together to show, but not to sell. I have seen fine exhibits of historical arms at these gun shows, of arms illustrating the evolution of the ignition systems, of the arms of a certain area or a particular gunmaking community. There are also frequent exhibits at these gun shows of the arms of a particular gun manufacturer, such as exhibits of a progression of Colts, Smith & Wessons, Marlins, Remingtons or Winchesters. Finally, there are fine shows which have won N.R.A. awards, such as Jim Smith's exhibit of revolving rifles or Harm Leonard's show of Colonial weapons. I have found interesting and informative displays of gamblers guns, crossbows, cane weapons, oddities and curiosa with signs saying "What is it?" and exhibits ranging from model cannon to miniatures.

Members of your local gun club who have been at the game of collecting longer than you will be helpful in telling and showing you about arms from their own collections. The pleasantest moments of my collecting career have been spent in the gun rooms of fellow collectors learning from them the nuances of their specialties and what to look for when buying a gun or sword.

There is so much to learn about the art of collecting that it won't fit in any one book. And there are many different directions one may take in becoming a collector. After you have seen representative collections of arms and have read about them, or at least have talked about them with knowledgeable collectors, you will know what field you want to enter. That is, if you are a born collector with an itch. There are some people who escape this urge and are quite content to sit under a palm tree and collect nothing but beautiful tropical sunsets.

Many years ago, when I was first thinking of becoming a serious collector, I was fascinated by combination weapons. These are guns combined with some other weapon or instrument. They could be a combination crossbow—wheel lock, a hunting sword with flintlock pistol barrels, or an American Elgin percussion pistol-cutlass combination of the nineteenth century.

My guide and teacher was a wonderful man who was the late armorer at the Metropolitan Museum of Art, Leonard Heinrich.

Leonard had not only worked as an armorer all of his life and was a real artist working in metal but he also had rare ability as a teacher. He could communicate, and he had the ability to inspire interest. At my request, Leonard taught me about early combination weapons from the many examples at the Metropolitan's collection and from photographs of combination weapons in European museums.

These very early combination weapons were almost always designed with the same thought in mind: if the primitive weapon, hand cannon, matchlock or early form of wheel lock failed to fire in an emergency the combination weapon could be used in some other way. I have seen combination crossbows and wheel-lock guns in Munich and one in Venice invented by Leonardo da Vinci; combination forked halberd and wheel-lock long gun (a gift of Henri II to the Doges); a court sword with a wheel-lock pistol concealed in its

Model of the combination wheel-lock halberds in the Palazzo Ducale Museum in Venice. The halberd shaft was also the gun barrel, the bullet emerging between the two fork blades of the halberd. These strange weapons were carried by the honor guard of the Venetian Doges. They were a present to the city of Venice from King Henri II of France.

jeweled hilt; and a series of horsemen's weapons, combinations of either axes or war hammers with wheel-lock guns. These are primitive weapons with a very early type of wheel-lock mechanism mounted externally on the lock plates, with the long mainsprings and sprocketed chains exposed. The Metropolitan has one such piece mounted on display in one of the side rooms behind the great armor hall. I had admired and studied the weapon, and Leonard had told me its history. It is an all-metal combination wheel lock and fighting axe made in Saxony or Nuremberg for a cuirassier of one of the Saxon princes and was made in the 1540s or '50s. Many years later, I was wandering through the gun show held at Stratford, Connecticut. It was not one of Stratford's best shows because the date coincided with the Ohio gun show. The Ohio show is much larger and more important than the Stratford show and most of the major dealers, collectors and exhibitors had chosen to go to Ohio. This left a smattering of small, local dealers and a hatful of guys selling spare parts, Nazi uniforms, die-cast replicas or arms, a few coins and mostly junk. I surveyed the room, munching on a cold hot dog and sipping some black coffee flavored with muriatic acid. I decided to give myself thirty minutes to case the entire show. If I found nothing in that time I would go home and repair an old gun. I scooted up one aisle and down the next, with eyes right, looking at as much as I could see without coming to a dead halt. I was three quarters of the way down the eighth and last aisle when I came to a dead halt. Here in front of me, on the table of an upstate dealer, mixed with a pile of percussion shotguns, was a companion of the wheel-lock–axe which hung in the Metropolitan.

If I hadn't seen the one in the Met, I would not have known what I was looking at because pictures in a book do not give you any sense of the scale of an object. I examined the piece as closely as I could without touching it. (It is always important to ask permission of a dealer or owner before picking up a piece.) I half expected to see the piece disappear or discover that what I was looking at was an optical illusion, but it wasn't. On the lock plate were two stamps, one of them quite distinct, of a rampant lion of Saxony. The ramrod was a replacement, but otherwise the all-steel piece was intact, including the cock, the cock jaws and screw. I inquired of the dealer, whom I knew

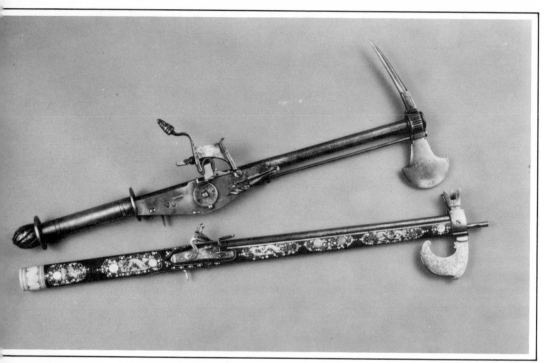

Two combination weapons. The upper one is a horseman's axe mounted on the shaft of a wheel-lock pistol. This all-metal arm has the stamp of the Saxon lion on the lock plate. The lower weapon is purely ceremonial and several hundred years later than the top gun. It is a fokos from Silesia. The flintlock gun would shoot, but the axe blade is shaped so that its utility is questionable.

by sight, what he could tell me about the weapon. He didn't know very much. It had come from an auction of the furnishings of a farmhouse in upstate Connecticut. The dealer didn't really know what the piece was except that it was crude and probably quite old. So, he had bought it, probably for not much money, since the auctioneer could not have been expected to know much about combination weapons either. The price the dealer was asking was, I am sure, high in comparison with what he had paid for it, but very cheap by my standards. I knew that one existed in the Metropolitan and probably no more than half a dozen in all of the museums in Europe. Needless to say I bought the arm on the spot without haggling over the price. I still have no idea how this mid-sixteenth-century German cavalryman's weapon came to be in a Connecticut farmhouse. My only thought is — and it's only a guess — that some G.I. who served in the van with Patton in World War II had liberated the piece from a provincial German museum or had bought it from a friendly Russian soldier on the German frontier.

The moral of this story is that you should learn all that you can about every weapon that you are near to, no matter how rare it may be. You can never tell when you may be standing next to a great bargain if you have the knowledge to recognize it.

If you become an advanced weapons collector, you will want to subscribe to the sale catalogs of Sotheby, Christie, Fischer and others. When you find in one of these sale catalogs a gun which looks interesting, what do you do? One thing you can do is to hop on the next jet to Europe, enjoy a vacation and attend the auction at the same time. If, however, you cannot afford either the time or the money, you can do the next best thing. You can pick an agent from a number of

Finely stocked wheel-lock gun by Michael Maucher, Munich stock maker. This weapon, now in the Tøjhus Museum in Copenhagen, has the figures of Venus and Cupid carved in ivory forming the patch box cover. To open the patch box, one presses on the ivory button that protrudes slightly from Venus's navel.

Rare Hans Stockmann double-barrel long pistol or carbine. This wheel lock has the characteristic Stockmann thin stock and lemon-shaped pommel.

reputable American and British arms dealers who make a business of attending all of these sales. Your agent will examine the piece first hand at the viewing before the sale. If he thinks the piece is any good, he will either bid for it if that is your instruction or he will check with you and advise you what he thinks that the piece will bring at the sale. Then you have to decide how much you want to spend if the bidding is competitive, and it always is these days. An agent will take a commission of from 5 to 10 percent depending on how expensive the arm is. Often your agent will save you more than his commission both by his advice and by knowing his way around the auction rooms. I, for one, would never trust myself to bid on my own account. I get too excited and would probably bid myself out of house and home. I went to a simple country auction once and bought a trunkload of wooden blocks and pulleys. It wasn't until the auctioneer pointed at me that I realized that I had been the person pushing up the bid. I still have lots of nice wooden pulleys in the barn to remind me not to go to auctions.

If you have a question about a gun that you want to buy but don't quite dare, make a deposit and borrow the gun for examination. Take it to a reputable dealer and ask his opinion. Most dealers are honest and will tell you what they know about the piece. Only remember to expect a certain amount of cold water to be thrown on it. It's only human nature not to like a piece as much if you don't own it or are not selling it at a profit.

Another way to find out about an old arm is to take it to the curator of arms and armor at your museum. Any curator worth his salt will try to give you as much information as he can. There are two *don'ts* to remember. Don't barge in on a curator and expect him to drop everything to look at your treasure. You are asking a favor and you should ask for an appointment at his convenience. The other thing to remember, no matter how much you want to, never ask a museum curator to put a dollar value on your piece. If you will stop to think, this is a very unfair question. There are a dozen reasons why you are putting him on the spot. You might be trying to sell the piece and use his name to support your price, or you might be buying a piece from a dealer who would not take it kindly to be told that so-and-so at the museum thought that the gun was only worth so much. An arms curator will, and should, help you in dating and identifying your piece, by telling you of its comparative rarity and condition. But from there, you have to arrive at the price that you want to put on it yourself. This can best be done by familiarizing yourself with auction and sale prices of similar pieces in the last few years. Let me repeat, *in the last few years*. For the last fifty years, firearms have doubled in value every ten years. In the last ten-year period, guns, along with all kinds of antiques, have tripled and in some cases quadrupled in value. A price that a gun sold for five years ago is a guide which must be upped by a large percentage.

I just became the owner of a pile of old auction catalogs. Old auction catalogs are a great help in tracing the provenance of a firearm. If the old catalogs are priced, they will show how the value of antique firearms has shot up from the past. In this particular pile was an Anderson Galleries catalog from November 1937. It was a sale of arms and armor in the estate of Theodore Offerman, who had been one of the founders of the Armor and Arms Club of New York. On page 77 of the catalog there is a picture of two wheel-lock pistols with very long barrels, number 366. On page 78 there is a description of the illustrated pair: "Pair Wheel-lock Pistols. German (Saxon) 1610. Of the State Guard of the Elector Christian II. Long dags with pear-shaped butts; stocks enriched with engraved bone. Barrels signed H.S. (Hans Stockmann, Dresden). From the Royal Armory, Dresden."

In the margin of the catalog, the price that these pistols brought has been noted in pencil. It was $220. These same pistols have been sold twice since then. In the most recent sale—about four years ago—they were purchased by a private collector in the United States for more than $20,000. In thirty-two years this particular pair of pistols has increased in value nearly a hundred times.

A note about rarity. Believe it or not, a firearm can be too rare to be of great value. If there are not very many pieces of a certain type of weapon in collections, or if the maker of the weapon is all but unknown, there will not be a very large group of collectors trying to buy the piece and, by bidding against each other, pushing up the price. A typical example of this occurred near my home. A very rare Cochran turret gun appeared at a local antique dealer's shop in Guilford, Connecticut. John Webster Cochran's turret guns have an odd cylinder made to revolve on a horizontal axis, versus a Colt cylinder turning on a vertical axis. They were being made for Cochran by C.B. Allen in Springfield, Massachusetts, at the same time that Samuel Colt was building his first revolvers in Paterson, New Jersey. The unusual-looking Cochran revolving rifles were well made but were produced in very small quantities and then production was discontinued entirely when the inventor went to Paris to patent a revolving cannon. The Cochran revolver is at least ten times as rare as the Colt Paterson revolving rifle, yet collectors not having seen a Cochran don't recognize it and won't pay half as much for it as they will for a

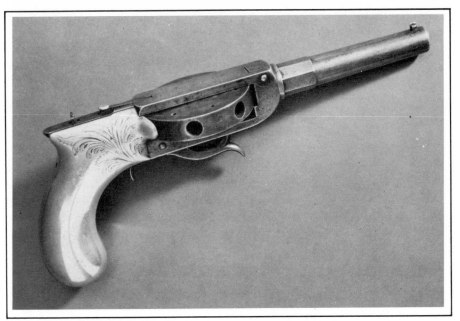

Cochran turret revolver with silver grips in the Winchester Gun Museum. Although much rarer than Colt revolvers of the same period, they do not bring as high prices, because not many people have seen them or know what they are.

Colt. If the Guilford dealer had had a Paterson Colt, it would have sold instantly for several thousand dollars. The Cochran hung on a peg in the antique dealer's shop for more than a year and was finally sold for a price of hundreds, not thousands of dollars.

Rarity alone, therefore, or age do not act as much in determining the value of a collectible firearm as does the current demand. If collectors know that Colts are valuable they will pay more for them than they will pay for older, rarer arms. As Colts have become increasingly hard to find and more and more expensive, collectors have turned to the study of other types of weapons. Today there is much more interest and knowledge of European weapons than there was twenty years ago. Beginning collectors have turned to them, driven off by the high prices of the better-known American weapons.

Once a general type of weapon has become established as a desirable one to collect — for example, a Colt Dragoon pistol — then small variations and markings can change the price of the piece in an extraordinary manner. A Dragoon with military markings is worth two or three times as much as a plain commercial model, and a

Dragoon with military markings which is also inscribed as having been presented to an officer by his men, or from anyone to anyone, with a date, is again worth several times more than the same arm with military markings alone. This, of course, has led arms fakers to inscribe plain Colt revolvers with inscriptions indicating that they were presented to some celebrity. Your only protection against such a forgery is a knowledge of the history of the piece and, particularly, the names of the previous owners. It will also help to know the dates of manufacture of a particular arm. Arms fakers are not always very good arms historians. I was once offered a Thuer conversion of the 1860 Colt New Model Army revolver. This pistol, which had seen better days, had once been engraved and gilt, but neglect and rust had destroyed most of the original finish, and small boys snapping the pistol had broken the hammer spring and some of the moving parts. In any event, the lamentable condition aside, this pistol was offered to me as the very gun that was used to execute the Emperor Maximilian of Mexico. In all likelihood, Maximilian was executed in a conventional manner by a firing squad with rifles, but no matter what weapon or weapons were used, this revolver wasn't there. Maximilian was executed on June 19, 1867, and Thuer was granted his patent on the cartridge conversion on September 15, 1868. Few Thuer conversions were actually made before 1869.

Rare weapons seldom have a sign on them stating their rarity or worth, age or historical importance. There are a number of collectors of arms who do not have the interest or the knowledge to track down the history of antique arms. For them, the arms industry has produced a series of commemorative reproductions. These will be the subject of the next chapter.

Reproductions

ARE MODERN COMMEMORATIVES
WORTH COLLECTING?

Arms and armor, matters of life or death to the user and wearer, have tended to be conservative. Frequently their design has reflected an earlier time than their actual manufacture. Two suits of parade armor in the Kunsthistorisches Museum in Vienna made in the 1500s in Milan are designed to look like something a Roman might have worn one hundred years before the birth of Christ. One suit, signed by the famous armorer Philip Negroli, was made in 1532 for Francesco Maria Rovere di Montefeltre of Urbino. The armor covering the body is in the shape of a short-sleeved shirt with a skirt. It is actually small overlapping plates sewn on fabric. It is known as a brigandine. In Roman times it was called squamata, for the fish scales it resembled. The helmet that goes with this armor is back hammered to resemble neatly curled locks of human hair, a treatment one sees in classical sculpture and one used decoratively in making helmets for Roman legionnaires before A.D. 250. We find this in fragments of helmets excavated at the Roman garrison town of Dura Europas which was destroyed in A.D. 262.

The other half suit of armor and a round shield to match were made for Archduke Ferdinand of the Tyrol around 1560. It was also produced in Milan, which was the great armor center, by Giovanni Batista Serabaglio. The body armor is made of a number of attached plates which articulate like a crawfish's shell. The short sleeves of the armor, similar to those worn by Roman legionnaires, end with scalloped tabs attached with rivets. The helmet with a visor, crest and ear flaps is an embossed version of a Corinthian helmet.

At the time of Napoleon, handguns and long guns made by the famous Boutet at the Versailles workshops were decorated with motifs of Greek and Roman times. Napoleon's cuirassiers wore completely useless breast and backplates, reminiscent of earlier functional armor, and carried ugly short swords imitating the gladius of the Roman gladiators. This fashion in arms was adopted in the United States, where the short, thick sword with its heavy bronze guard was worn with the dress uniforms by officers in the 1805-1820 era.

Double-cased pairs of Boutet pistols made for Napoleon I. These so-called traveling pistols are decorated in red gold, yellow gold, and cut steel. The plainer pair, with 288 gold stars inlaid in each barrel, were presumably designed for everyday use, and the fully encrusted pair were for state affairs. Neither pair seems ever to have been shot. The decorative motifs, including sphinxes, commemorate Napoleon's Egyptian campaign.

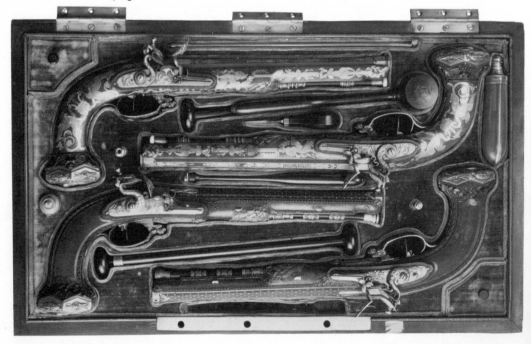

Detail of an ivory hunting horn. This horn, carved in Dieppe, France, in the early years of the nineteenth century is a skillful adaptation of Cellini's nymph of Fountainbleu. Details of the horn reproduce the combined cartouche of Henri II and his mistress Diane de Poitiers.

As the nineteenth century progressed and a widespread interest in antique arms created a demand, craftsmen made guns and pistols, powder horns and accouterments imitating earlier periods. Many of these reproductions were expertly made and command high prices today. Among such desirable pieces are miniature wheel-lock pistols made at the order of the German princes and used as souvenirs at state dinners, weddings, and coronations. Other rare and valuable reproductions are the ivory powder and hunting horns expertly and intricately carved at Dieppe with the insignia of ancient royalty. These are so well made that I have seen them proudly displayed in museums as works of the seventeenth not the nineteenth century.

Toward the end of the nineteenth century armorers Ernst Schmidt of Munich, G. Pigeon of Paris, and craftsmen of Berlin and Vienna undertook to satisfy the new market for reproduction armor. Well-to-do businessmen who had built homes copying Gothic originals needed a suit of armor, a two-handed sword or a crossed pair of highly decorated wheel-lock pistols to share the front hall with an umbrella stand and a Victorian coat rack. Everything was available from Schmidt, from full-size cannon of archaic form to flintlock pistols which sold for eight marks. Schmidt was not trying to fool anybody into thinking his arms were old. He published a catalog showing the pieces he made and listing prices and where the original was that he had copied. He marked his pieces with the date and either his name or the name of the craftsman who had made it.

Some of these Schmidt pieces were well enough made to fool experts. Today clearly identified as Schmidt's work, they bring thousands of dollars when they are sold. The quality of Schmidt's workshop production is illustrated by this incident. James Rorimer, director of the Metropolitan Museum of Art, came into the armor workshop of the museum where Leonard Heinrich was restoring a shirt of chain mail. Rorimer interrupted Heinrich's work to show him a Gothic candlestick made of brass or latten. Heinrich recognized the workmanship on the candlestick and, wishing to be tactful, asked Rorimer if the object had been given to the museum. Rorimer said that he had personally bought the Gothic candlestick at a well-known gallery in Switzerland. Leonard asked Rorimer for permission to take it apart, which Rorimer told him he could do, but cautioned him to be gentle, as the piece was old and delicate. Leonard mumbled that the piece was not as delicate as it looked and proceeded to take it apart. Once he had unscrewed the stem from the base, Leonard was able to show the boss his own signature and the date, 1911, engraved on the base. Two years later, Rorimer told Heinrich that he had gotten the museum's money back from the Swiss art gallery.

Quantity reproduction of historic arms and weapons of the past really got underway in the past thirty years with the manufacture by Sturm Ruger of their version of the Frontier single-action revolver. Colt, who had made the weapon in a variety of calibers from 1873 until World War II, decided that the single-action army revolver had run out its lifespan and was no longer in sufficient demand to be continued in the line. Colt management could not have made a bigger mistake. Colt stopped just at the time when popular interest in western arms had started to peak. For a number of years, Sturm Ruger had orders for more single-action Frontier 22-caliber pistols than they could manufacture. Finally Colt recognized the error of their ways and went back into production of the old gun which has not changed appreciably in a hundred years.

The most popular and enduring of all of the guns ever manufactured by the Winchester Repeating Arms Company is the model 1894 lever-action rifle and carbine invented by John Browning. Several million of these popular deer rifles had been manufactured and sold by the time Winchester was approaching its centennial. The brass at

Engraved and gold-inlaid commemorative single-action Colt .45 revolvers. This "Lawman Commemorative" illustrates the life of Pat Garrett. It was engraved and inlaid by master engraver Alvin White.

the Winchester Company gave a lot of thought to the question of what would be timely and appropriate to manufacture for their hundredth birthday. First, it was to make a centennial reissue of the original Winchester, the model 1866. After an expenditure of tens of thousands of dollars and more than a year's time, the designers at Winchester discovered what old Oliver Winchester had figured out nearly a century ago: the 1866 was a lousy gun that shot a weak cartridge. Oliver's engineers had strengthened the action and improved the cartridge and brought out the Winchester model 1873. The Winchester management in 1966 experimented with a reissue of the 1866 and concluded that such a gun would not only be unpopular today but that it could not be expected to contain powerful, smokeless loads. They settled on a perfectly safe choice, the ever-popular 1894. The centennial model, suitably inscribed 1866 - 1966, was nothing but the old reliable 1894 gussied up with some plating and engraving.

The commemorative market was explored cautiously by the Winchester Company in this first model. Initially about twenty thousand were scheduled for manufacture, but before the centennial model was discontinued, more than one hundred thousand had been

Not a reproduction but a continuation of the 1851 square back series reinstituted in the Colt Line in 1973. The scroll engraving is by the A.A. White engraving group.

World War II Air Force commemorative .45 automatic Colt. This pistol, which belongs to the president of Colt Firearms, is similar to but fancier than the Colt .45 series of World War I commemoratives.

Winchester Buffalo Bill Commemorative.

made. Winchester knew a good thing when it hit, especially since the decorated commemorative sold for approximately $40 more than the standard model 1894. Only a Winchester commemorative buff could list all of the commemorative versions which Winchester proceeded to issue. They were all the 1894 actions to which a certain amount of cosmetic treatment had been applied. Commemorative Winchesters sold as many as a hundred and fifty thousand of individual issues such as the Buffalo Bill, the Cowboy Hall of Fame, the Teddy Roosevelt, the Canadian Mounties, the Texas Ranger, and on and on and on.

Collectors often bought these guns as investments. As Winchester issued each new model, they bought the new commemoratives in both rifle and carbine lengths and tried to get as low serial numbers as possible, stowing the guns away in their original factory shipping cartons. Some of these collectors did very well, especially those who bought the early commemorative models. In time, however, Winchester out-produced the commemorative market and the later guns began to accumulate not in collectors' closets or gun room walls but in hardware dealers' warehouses. Winchester was finally forced to stop issuing them and is now sticking to the manufacture of hunting and target weapons. The collectors who bought these commemoratives across the board have made out well on the average. The early models doubled and tripled in value and the later models have about held their own. Anyone who has held on to the whole series and who is willing to wait until the last of the commemoratives issued by Winchester is at least ten years old will probably do extremely well.

Colt Patent Firearms got into the manufacturing of commemorative arms on a more modest scale. One of their series has been the 1911 model Colt military 45 automatic also designed by John Browning. The Colt series, commemorating the major battles of World War I, were engraved with the names Château Thierry, Somme, Marne, Meuse-Argonne, etc. The quantities of these weapons ran between two thousand five hundred and five thousand. Because the quantities were smaller, the commemorative collectors got a better break. Some of these Colts have reached the astronomical price of $2,500.

Colt has now reissued the 1873 single-action Frontier in two sizes and finishes and ninety different models. They are marketing, singly and in pairs, reproductions of the Colt 3rd model (Thuer) derringer in 22 caliber instead of the original 41 caliber. The other Colt commemorative is the 1851 Navy percussion revolver. For Civil War buffs, it is available in either a U.S. Grant or a Robert E. Lee model at $150. Colt is also making the famous Dragoon, but they do not consider it to be a commemorative. It is not being produced in a limited edition. Instead, the numbers continue from 20,900, which is where they left off in 1847.

Although not a gun, the tomahawk issued by the Texas Rangers Sesquicentennial Commission will interest arms collectors. Five hundred hand-engraved, silver-plated, serial-numbered tomahawks made by R. W. Wilson are being sold for $215 a throw.

Smith & Wesson has its own Texas Ranger commemorative. It is a .357 magnum double-action revolver with a cut-out trigger guard for rapid fire. It comes cased with a bowie knife. The pistol has a Texas Rangers' badge roll-engraved on the side plate.

Marlin has issued two commemoratives. One is a Zane Grey 30/30 carbine and the other, which came out in 1961, commemorated their own ninetieth anniversary in the arms industry.

Remington commemorative models include Ducks Unlimited shotguns and a Montana Territorial Centennial Model 600 rifle issued in 1964.

Ithaca brought out a St. Louis Bicentennial 22-caliber rifle model 49; Ruger, a Canadian Centennial 22-caliber rifle; and Harrington and Richardson, another 22, this time a revolver celebrating the Abilene Centennial.

Savage Arms issued a commemorative model 99 rifle to celebrate their own seventy-fifth year in business, while Harrington and Richardson has reproduced a genuine antique shooter, the Officers' Model 45-70 trap-door Springfield.

The Hi Standard Manufacturing Company in Hamden, Connecticut, makes, among others things, 22 target pistols. They chose to make a presentation Olympic model 22 target pistol inlaid with gold and cased in walnut.

Two factors are contributing to the enormous growth of interest in reproduction black-powder muzzle-loaders in both flint and percussion. The restrictions on the ownership of modern cartridge guns has made many a collector and shooter turn to black-powder shooting and the home building of firearms from plans or from kits. The other factor is the growing interest in conservation of all kinds. With all forms of wildlife diminishing, high-powered, multi-shot magazine or automatic weapons seem less and less sporting or desirable. A hunter who goes into the woods armed with a single-shot black-powder gun is not going to bring home the bacon unless he is a better woodsman and a better shot than a guy equipped with a scoped, magazine hunting rifle. Also, to date, I have not heard of a single bank robbery, stick up or murder being committed with either a flintlock or a percussion arm. This is why there are practically no restrictions on their ownership or use.

A great number of manufacturers and mail-order gun dealers have specialized in selling black-powder reproduction arms and kits to make these arms. Any of the gun magazines will provide you with a list of them and the products they sell. Many have catalogs and most of them have moderately priced kits which can produce just as fine reproduction arm as you have the patience to make and finish.

A sampling of some of the well-established black-powder arms producers and their wares turns up the following firms, listed alphabetically.

Centennial Arms in Lincolnwood, Illinois, sells a number of kits, starting with a reproduction of a British Tower flintlock pistol for the low price of $24.95, and ranging to $500 for an exact copy of the North and Cheney pistol in a numbered edition of 100.

Connecticut Valley Arms in Haddam, Connecticut, has a catalog which includes kits and built-up models of Colonial pistols, flintlock long guns and New Model Army revolvers.

Dixie Gun Works in Union City, Tennessee, puts out a 400-page catalog of gun parts, kits for building antique reproductions, and also for making modern muzzle-loading shooters.

E.M.F. in Studio City, California, list 1851 Colt Navy's and presentation cased sets from $63. In order to maintain any quality at all at prices like these, the parts have to have been manufactured abroad, and indeed, most of the more moderately priced kits are made in Japan, Italy and Belgium. Even then, the quality cannot be outstanding on the simplest arm priced under $100.

Federal Ordnance in South El Monte, California, is making a 44-caliber Remington army revolver.

Golden Age Arms Company in Worthington, Ohio, sells both flintlock and percussion Kentucky rifle and pistol kits as well as do-it-yourself powder horn and tomahawk kits.

Lyman Gunsight in Middlefield, Connecticut, is an old and well-established firm making not only iron and telescopic sights but hand-loading tools of all descriptions. They have recently entered the commemorative black-powder field with a percussion plains rifle shooting minie balls. The arm sells for $193.

Navy Arms Corp. in Ridgefield, New Jersey, puts out a four-color catalog of historical reproductions including a 58-caliber Hawken percussion rifle at $175.

Numrich Arms Corp. in West Hurley, New York, offers a Pennsylvania rifle kit for $109.50, and Buffalo rifle and Creedmore kits based on the rolling block Remington action for the low price of $44.50.

All of these companies, and many more whose names I do not know, try to produce kits and built-up arms at a reasonable price to attract the greatest number of buyers. I wish some of them would try for a better product at higher prices.

At the other end of the stick there are quality arms produced in very limited numbers. The workmanship is of the best quality, but, alas, the prices of these pieces reflect the high cost of handwork of any kind.

In Williamsburg, Virginia, gunsmith Wallace Gusler hand-makes superb Kentucky rifles in the same manner they were made two hundred years ago. At the gun shop which has been reconstructed at Colonial Williamsburg you can watch Gusler or his assistants make a complete working gun from a block of figured maple and some bits of rusty iron. Each lock part is cut out, filed and shaped by hand, work which the Kentucky makers during Revolutionary days could do but preferred not to, if they could buy ready-made locks imported from Birmingham or Liège. The stock is inletted by hand to hold the lock and barrel. The wood is also cut away exactly to receive the furniture consisting of a side plate, butt plate and returns, trigger guard, barrel pin escutcheons and any of a number of decorative silver inlays which the customer may specify or which would be appropriate for the chosen period of the weapon.

The hardest job of all, and one of the first to be undertaken in the making of the complete Kentucky, is the barrel itself. The barrel is made the old-fashioned way by taking six or seven shovel-shaped billets or pieces of iron called skelps and heating and hammering them to make one continuous sleeve around an iron mandrel. At first the heating and hammering flattens the individual pieces which are folded and hammered and heated some more. This is accompanied by constantly scraping off the scurf which forms on the surface and contains impurities from the iron. The heating and hammering process give a toughness and a grain to the iron which with skillful forging comes together in one piece. One of the problems in making a barrel in this manner is the tendency of the tube to stick to the mandrel. Once the rough tube is in one piece securely and tightly welded so that no seam exists, the tube is bored out to make it smooth. When it is straight and smooth and the right diameter, the barrel is locked in position in the rifling machine. From here it is rifled one groove at a time by a hand-turned tool which is inserted into the beginning of the barrel. It cuts a spiral groove dictated by the threads cut in the axle of the wooden rifling tool. When the rifling is cut, normally six of seven grooves, it is ready to be polished on the inside and fitted with barrel pin lugs, a breech plug and tang and a front sight. The barrel is then drilled for a touch hole, inlet into the stock and polished bright and blued. The whole job of making a single barrel by hand takes a skilled gunsmith like Gussler weeks to complete. Of course, in the early days of the Kentucky rifle, barrels were made presumably more than one at a time and some of the work was done by apprentices under the watchful eye of the master gunsmith. The final barrel, more than any other gun part, was what the gunsmith was judged by. Its straightness and the gun's ability to shoot accurately were what counted. The men who made the best barrels often set up small factory operations and sold barrels to other gunsmiths.

When Wally finishes a Kentucky rifle it is unique and a true work of art. The value of such a piece, though high to begin with, can only go up, as there are but a handful of skilled craftsmen who can and are willing to do this hard and demanding work. One last thing about this

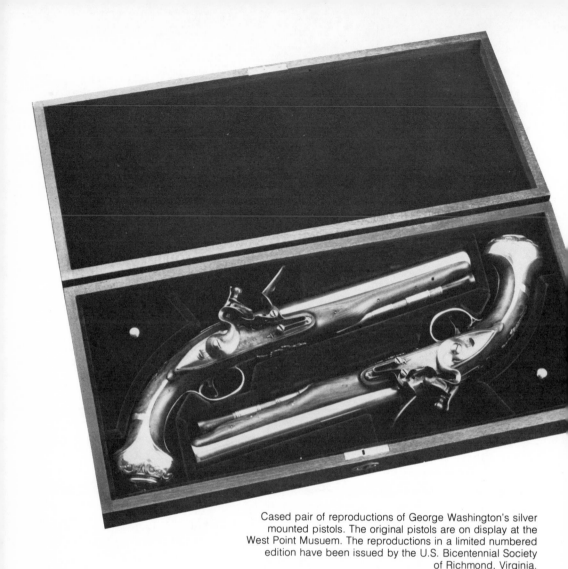

Cased pair of reproductions of George Washington's silver mounted pistols. The original pistols are on display at the West Point Musuem. The reproductions in a limited numbered edition have been issued by the U.S. Bicentennial Society of Richmond, Virginia.

type of gunsmithing: don't be in a hurry when you order such a rifle from Wally or one of the other Kentucky makers. They can make only a few rifles a year and if they are any good at all, they are back-ordered for two or three years.

Another type of historical commemorative has made its appearance with the Bicentennial of the United States. The U.S. Bicentennial Society, a group of noted historians and businessmen in Richmond, Virginia, have commissioned, among other things, the exact reproduction of a pair of George Washington's pistols. The original pistols are in the West Point Museum. With the permission of the museum director Richard Kuehne, exact casts, drawing and photographs were made of the original pistols. The Washington pistols are quite elaborate, having seven sterling-silver fittings including grotesque mask butt plates, an elaborate panoply of arms in relief on the side plate, engraved and beaded silver trigger guard and ramrod thimbles and a sterling escutcheon plate in the thumb position in the form of the head of a satyr with a beard.

The original pistols, made in London in 1748-1749 by Richard Wilson and John Hawkins, both "Masters of the Worshipful Company of Gunmakers," are examples of the best quality of British gunsmithing. The reproductions, in a numbered edition of one thousand, are handmade and proofed in exactly the same manner as the originals, and fashioned out of bronze cannon metal, steel, sterling silver and the finest French walnut. The pistols are sold by the U.S. Bicentennial Society for $2,500 the cased pair.

This same Bicentennial group is also reproducing the pair of Wogdon pistols which were used in the duel between Aaron Burr and Alexander Hamilton in which the latter was fatally wounded. The

Cased pair of the Wogdon pistols with which Aaron Burr shot Alexander Hamilton. The original pistols are in the vaults of the Chase Manhattan Bank. These have been reproduced for the bicentennial by the U.S. Bicentennial Society of Richmond.

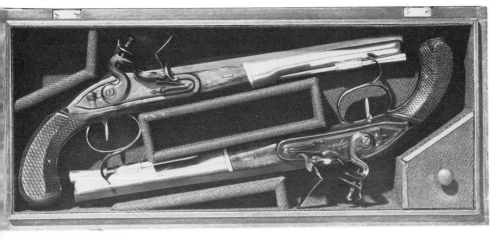

pistols, though plain, are the best quality English duellers of the late 1700s. They have quite a history, having been used in three famous duels. The pistols belonged to John Barker Church, who was Hamilton's brother-in-law. They were first used in a duel between Church and Aaron Burr in which no one was injured. Then they were used in a duel by Hamilton's son in which he was killed. Finally they were supplied by Church for the Burr-Hamilton duel at Weehawken. The pistols remained in the Church family until they were purchased by the Chase Manhattan Bank, an organization which was founded by Aaron Burr and whose existence was a threat to the Hamilton-sponsored Bank of the United States. The Chase Manhattan Bank and the U.S. Bicentennial Society are jointly sponsoring the issue of these commemoratives.

Both the Washington and the Burr-Hamilton pistols are valuable as limited editions of commemorative arms and as fine examples of these historic weapons.

Whether you elect to collect commemorative reproductions or antique originals, you must take the necessary steps to protect your weapons. If you don't, the steel will rust and the finish will suffer. This will not only reduce the value of your collection but it will also spoil the pleasure of having a display of good-looking arms. Care of the guns that you own is the subject of Chapter 10.

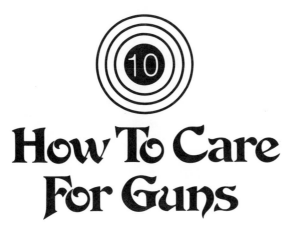

How To Care
For Guns

DIRT CAN MESS UP YOUR COLLECTION

Firearms are not the easiest things in the world to care for. If you want something easy, I suggest you collect coins, china or glassware. There are lots of coins in fine condition which were struck in Greek and Roman times, but few hand firearms which predate 1450. And these are in pretty horrible condition. Five-hundred-year-old arms that survive usually have bronze barrels—and that is all that is left of them. We know from manuscript illustration and documents that there were hand firearms from early 1300s. But the oldest examples surviving are from later years—the Loshult vase gun made around 1350; the Tannenberg gun, possibly as old as 1399; a bronze Hackenbuchse (hand cannon with a hook) in the museum in Hildesheim, Germany, made before 1450; the Vedelspang gun, *circa* 1400, in Copenhagen; the bronze barrel of a hand cannon in the Artillery Museum in Turin, Italy; and the Berne, Switzerland, hand cannon from 1375. Only the metal parts of them has survived. These oldest guns were pretty crude in construction and were not cared for as works of art or as useful tools. As a matter of fact, the method of

119

William Renwick's Maximilian gun now in the Smithsonian Institution. It may be the earliest surviving rifled arm. Before conservation it was so wormed that the stock weighed and felt like cork.

Combination wheel lock and crossbow belonging to the Archduke Ferdinand of the Netherlands. The weapon, which is dateable to the 1520s, is missing the dog's head which held the pyrites. It could not be restored correctly, because no one knows exactly what it looked like.

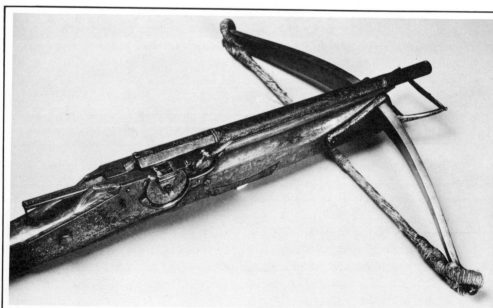

arriving at an educated guess as to the date of their manufacture is based on archaeological procedures. The various barrels were excavated from earth layers containing datable objects, or they have been found under the ruins of castles known to have been destroyed at a certain time.

Surviving wooden stocks do not occur on arms made much before 1500, and then only on early matchlocks. The first crossbow—wheel lock, which can be dated around 1510 with the da Vinci lock in the Palazzo Ducale in Venice, has an iron stock, and the second, with a coat of arms and signature dating it to 1521, in the Bavarian National Museum in Munich, is stocked in wood. This painted wooden stock, being on a royal weapon, has survived in fair shape. The lockless gun of Henry VIII was subjected to the dampness of the Tower of London, and the Maximilian gun in the Renwick collection was subjected to God knows what tribulations. They are nothing but wormy scraps of wood now. Since Bruce Pendleton photographed the Renwick rifle, one of the packers picked up the arm a bit roughly and it broke in two. Fortunately, Maximilian's coat of arms, which is painted on both sides of the weapon, was not affected and the stock, with care, can be put back together.

Before a disaster like this happens to you, let me advise you about the care of wormed stocks and stocks which have been affected by dry rot, mildew or damp. First, the metal parts of the gun should be removed with the greatest caution. If the wood is corky or crumbly do not force anything, but treat wood and metal together. Ideally, the wood should be exposed to cyanide gas which will destroy both worms and microorganisms. Cyanide, however, is lethal to human beings and is not to be used experimentally by amateurs. If you are not a chemist or do not have the equipment to contain the gas safely, the next best way to arrest deterioration of the wood is to soak it in any powerful insecticide. I use a termite poison, a ten percent solution of chlordane, and, depending on the size of the stock, I either paint on the clear aqueous solution with a soft brush or soak the stock if I have a container large enough. Overnight soaking or several paintings will do the trick. Then a coat of Cuprinol will inhibit cracking or dry rot. When the wood is good and dry so that it will not hold moisture next to metal parts, the restoration of the stock can be undertaken.

If the stock is wormed to the point of being spongy, the job is tedious but necessary. Get a horse hypodermic needle and syringe from your local vet or from a surgical supply house and make a slow-drying mixture of epoxy, colored to match the wood. The solution of epoxy can be applied by filling the individual holes with the hypodermic syringe. If the holes are large it may take two applications to fill them level because the epoxy will sink in and leave a dimple on the surface. If care is used, and each worm hole is filled, the stock will not only look the way that it was intended but it will be a hundred times stronger. With epoxy filling all the holes, the stock will be strong enough to support the barrel and lock. I have known badly wormed stocks to double in weight from the added epoxy. When the epoxy has set and smoothed to the surface of the wood with 0000 steel wool, the entire surface can be painted with minwax antique oil finish and then polished with a hard wax such as Butchers wax or Simoniz.

Some museum restorers will object violently to my use of epoxy on the theory that nothing should be added to an antique which cannot be removed. I have seen the restoration work of the woodwork repairer at the Rijksmuseum in Amsterdam. He uses only hard wax to replace missing wood pieces and he is able to duplicate missing wood grains exactly. I have even seen him inlay mother-of-pearl in the wax base of a Dutch wheel-lock repair. This is all very well if the restored piece is going to repose in a glass case and never be handled except by the restorer, but a piece that is going to hang on the wall of a gun room wouldn't last for two minutes if restored with wax.

French wheel-lock pistol by F. Duclos, circa 1635. From the Barron Cossen and the Duc de Dino collections, now Metropolitan Museum No. 04.3192, The screw missing from the side plate could and has been replaced, since others like it survived on the gun.

All of which leads to another ticklish question, that is, how much restoration is necessary or desirable. Some museum curators and conservationists claim that nothing should be done to change the condition of a firearm from the way it was when they first saw it. In other words, if a screw falls out, the gun should be left that way. If five minutes before the curator first saw the arm someone dropped it on the floor and broke the stock, it should not be repaired. I think that this is pure hokum and also suspect that many of the advocates of this school are simply bone lazy.

I believe that damage or repairs made to a weapon during its working life—a stock lengthened, a sleeve put over the throat of a cracked Kentucky, or any of a number of possible repairs which would make a weapon serviceable—should be left alone. I believe that dirt which has accumulated while the weapon has been in a collection, or rust from fingerprints should be removed, that missing screws should be replaced, bits of inlay which have fallen out should be reglued, springs or cock necks which have been broken by idiots snapping locks should be remade or repaired. As a basic rule, restoration should be done to correct any recent damage to an old weapon as long as that repair does not destroy any of the original finish. If the removal of a bit of rust will take with it a fire-gilt design on the surface of a barrel, either leave the rust or figure out some other method of restoration.

Guns should be cleaned periodically whether they are new or old. Dust accumulating on the iron and steel parts has a tendency to retain moisture from the air. The minute amount of water trapped by the dust and held on the surface of the arm will eventually rust the piece. Another constant problem is finger-printing. Some people have more acid perspiration than others, and they can rust a gun by merely touching it with an apparently dry hand. For this reason, never handle another man's guns without first asking permission, and then try to avoid touching the metal parts.

Some collectors protect their guns by keeping them in cases. Glass cases do cut down on the amount of airborne dust which can settle on an object and they do prevent fools from handling your prize pieces with wet hands. But they reduce the pleasure of having your collection fully examinable and pick-upable, with the right precautions. I personally do not like glass cases except for miniature arms, which should not be handled anyway without proper preparation: a felt pad and a magnifying glass and tweezers. Gloves are one solution. I keep a couple of pairs of light work gloves in my gun room and offer them to my guests who are interested in arms and care to examine or handle them. Many other collectors do the same. I have heard a tale that collector Otto von Kienbusch ordered the entire membership of the Armor and Arms Club of New York out of his Armor Hall after observing one of the members pick up a sword without first putting on the white cotton gloves he had provided.

If your guests don't take the hint, or you are too polite to explain what the gloves are for, the next best thing to do is to spend an hour or more after the guests have left, wiping off each piece you suspect has been handled. The problem is that if you do not wipe off every single piece in your collection, you will inevitably find that a gun up on the top shelf that you did not suspect had been handled has a nifty set of red, rusty fingerprints on the bright steel barrel. When you clean up after guests, first wipe the arms with a dry, soft cloth to remove all dust and moisture. Then spray the pieces lightly with one of the good aerosol gun or fishing-reel sprays. Do not aim the nozzle at the wood stocks or grips. And wipe off any visible accumulation of the spray from wood or ivory surfaces.

The best procedure of all, gloves or no gloves, is to protect your collection in advance, not only from handling by guests but also from general exposure to heat, humidity, dryness and dust. You should clean your entire collection at least once a year in the following manner. Spread newspapers over tables where the collection can be laid out. Place each arm on the paper, being sure that it doesn't hit or touch another. Now, clean the hangers, cases, mounts, racks where the arms are displayed. As a matter of fact, this is a good time to clean the gun room thoroughly to get rid of as much dust as possible.

Next, take a soft, dry rag. Cotton flannel is perfect, but old pieces of sheet or towel will do. Don't use turkish toweling because the loops of thread will hook themselves over metal parts. Wipe each piece clean. If excessive dust has accumulated, take a dry patch over a ramrod tip and clean the dust accumulation out of the bore. Use an old toothbrush to get into corners and tight places such as under the

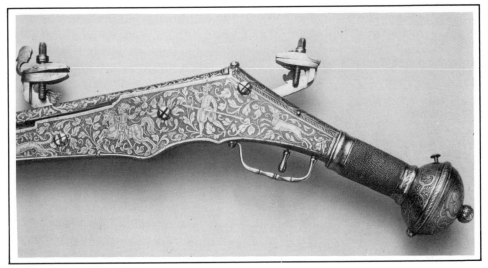

Abrasion is the worst enemy to acid etching of steel surfaces and the windings of wire on grips of both swords and guns. Wire grips can be rewound by a professional, but once the acid-etched design has been polished away, there is no way to restore it without doing further damage to the piece.

trigger guard or where the hammer fits into the frame of a modern revolver. As you clean the guns, observe them minutely, don't just wipe blindly. If you see the slightest spot of rust you must remove it with 0000 steel wool. Don't use coarser wool or kitchen Brillo, because this will scratch and wreck the surface you are trying to protect. If there is a persistent spot of rust which the 0000 steel wool will not remove, take anything made of copper or brass—a penny or a cartridge case will do—and scrape away the offending oxide. Copper or brass, being softer metal than iron or steel, can do no damage to the harder metal surface and will not remove bluing. But it will get the rust.

When your entire collection has been dry cleaned, spray exposed moving parts very gingerly with aerosol gun spray, keeping it off the wood. If you live in a very dry climate or your gun room is overheated in the winter time with no humidity control, it wil be a good idea to treat the wood with a first-rate furniture polish such as lemon oil or Vernax or one of the preparations designed for antique furniture. Again, don't splash the wood-protective material over the metal parts.

The final step is to coat the entire weapon with Butchers wax, bowling alley wax or Simoniz and then polish the pieces with a dry cloth after letting the wax dry for five minutes. Remove any excess wax from the barrel or crevices. This will leave your guns protected with a hard, attractive surface against moisture and casual handling. The finish you have applied will last for a year except in extremes of climate where the arms are exposed to lots of moisture, salt air on the ocean, intense heat on the desert, or in the direct draft of a hot-air furnace.

If your collection is unavoidably going to be exposed to any of these extremes, you may have to consider some type of climate control. Adding humidity where needed is the easiest. Complete control of dust and moisture will require an air-conditioned home or gun room. If air-conditioning is the solution, watch it carefully and check with a humidity indicator the areas where your guns are kept. Too much moisture or too little moisture can warp wood or ivory stocks and cook or rot leather. The leather can be protected by British Museum leather dressing and the stocks, to a certain degree, by the methods of cleaning and maintenance I have described. But curing the effects of exposure to extremes of moisture or dryness does not always work, and is a long, slow process that is best avoided.

The collection which suffered worst from extremes of weather and neglect was the William Renwick armory. Bill Renwick was a great arms scholar and put together over many years the finest and most exciting private collection of firearms in America. But Bill wasn't a good housekeeper. As near as I could tell, and I handled and examined each of the 1,765 arms he had collected, he never cleaned a gun in his collection. If he bought a dirty gun it stayed dirty. If he bought a clean gun it got dirty. At first Renwick lived in Weston, Massachusetts, where the collection, housed on the inshore side of Boston and not too far removed from Massachusetts Bay, was subjected to a lot of moisture. There is no salt sea air in Weston, and while this area of Massachusetts is subject to damp spells, normal cleaning and oiling or waxing would have prevented the rust that started to form on Renwick's guns.

Rather than clean the guns, Renwick moved them to a home he built in Tucson, Arizona, where the arms were subjected to the oppo-

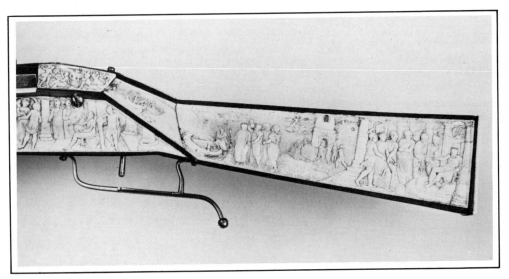

Ivory used in the decoration of arms, especially such large carved panels as these, can easily be ruined with too much heat and too little humidity.

Ivory inlays can pop out due to failure of the old glue or through shrinkage of the wood of the stock in steam-heated homes. Replace the inlays with a soluble glue before they are lost.

site extreme. His house was located right out on the desert. Even though his specially built gun room was air-conditioned, the wood, bone, horn and ivory stocks started to shrink and warp. Inlays from priceless antique wheel-lock guns fell out on the floor and were swept up and in some cases thrown away. Bill was a charming and gracious host who used to give an occasional party in his gun room. He was much too polite to ask his guests not to handle his guns, and the result was that many fine weapons in the collection were covered with red, rusty fingerprints from the hands of guests who had set down drinks and, with moist hands, had picked up guns.

Part of the Renwick collection was given to the Smithsonian Institution in Washington, D.C., a part of the world not noted for its healthful climate. Natives sometimes refer to Washington as foggy bottom in describing the rainy, humid climate that hangs like a pall over the portion of the city bordering on the Potomac River. That is precisely where the Smithsonian is located. Smithsonian Curator, Dr. Craddock Goins, had two monumental jobs on his hands when he received the Renwick bequest. The first was to overcome the damage done to the guns by years of neglect. The second job was to bring the moisture-starved stocks back gradually to a proper water content without having them break completely or warp away from the metal.

It took the conservation department of the museum over three years to feed moisture back into the wood of the Renwick arms. The pieces were placed in watertight bags and given increasing doses of moisture so that over a period of time they would gradually adjust to the conditions which exist in the Smithsonian Institution's Museum of Science and Industry where the Renwick Collection is displayed.

There are many little tricks I have learned over the years that will help you keep your gun collection in tip-top condition. The bluing on a modern gun is applied by the gunsmith or factory to protect the arm from rust. Bluing isn't foolproof, but it does help. If through holster wear, or previous polishing, some of the bluing has been rubbed off but the surface is smooth, it is easy to blacken the bright surface spot with cold blue. Any gun shop and most hardware stores will sell you a little plastic bottle of gun blue for a couple of dollars which will last you a long time. One of the more versatile brands in called 44/40 Instant Gun Blue, but you may want to experiment to find the blue that will most nearly match the color of your gun. Cold blue is simple to apply. Just take a little piece of cotton and wipe it on the bright steel which you have previously cleaned with alcohol to remove grease or dirt. The blue will appear instantly. Wipe the piece dry and then wax the surface to protect the blue. Be careful whenever you wax a gun not to leave wax in the bore. It looks bad, collects dirt, and if the gun is a shooter it could cause real trouble.

In selecting a cold chemical blue, do not buy blue paint or enamel or a preparation with a name like "new blue." When applied to gun parts it looks like paint, which is horrible.

If you have a silver-plated weapon which has had the silver rubbed off of small areas, it can be restored with silver-plating liquid which contains pure silver particles in a liquid suspension. Shake the bottle and apply with a bit of cotton in the same way you apply cold blue. In either case, do not get it on your skin. If your skin is apt to be sensitive, wear a cheap throw-away plastic glove on the hand holding the cotton. Single gloves which fit either hand are sold at hardware stores for pennies.

If an old gun has been engraved and gilt and traces of gliding remain to show where the fire gilt was applied, a gold surface effect can be recreated by using Liquid Leaf. This preparation, sold in art supply stores, comes in yellow gold and reddish Florentine gold.

I have purposely not gone into the gun-cleaning procedures you should follow if you are a hunter. These rules come with every new gun. If you have an old gun which is filthy, with crud and rust in the lock and barrel, clean it first with Hoppe's to remove the caked crud, which is the black-powder residual. Then use fine steel wool to

The pistol shield used by Henry VIII's guards. These were used in the defense of the Tower of London. This one in the Joe Kindig Collection has been over-cleaned and shows only bright metal segments around the breech-loading matchlock pistol barrel. Other surviving shields still in the Tower show traces of gilding.

remove any rust, taking care not to leave any broken-off hairs of the wool in the lock cavity to rust again. If the bare metal parts are still rusty and dirty, you may have to resort to a wire brush, preferably copper or brass wire, and Zud, a powdered cleanser which works on bare metal if applied with plenty of elbow grease. Zud will remove hard rust and some metal stains. When two working (or moving) pieces of a lock or a screw in a lock or side plate are rusted-in solid so that they will not move, soak the screw head and shaft or the rusted lock parts with Liquid Wrench or kerosene. Liquid Wrench works better and faster for me. After a half hour and several applications, start to tap the pieces that are rusted together. Use a wooden mallet, a lead or thong hammer so that you will not damage or malform the old iron of the screw or part. After a couple of taps, pour on more Liquid Wrench; the jarring of the piece by tapping will have opened a crevice which will allow the solvent to flow between the pieces. Don't be impatient. Give the liquid a minute or two more to penetrate the rust and then start tapping again. If it is a frozen screw, insert the right-sized screwdriver in the slot and tap the screwdriver in the right direction, taking great pains not to deface the slot. This will work in nine cases out of ten. In the tenth case the rust may have gone so far that there is no metal left and the screw will break in two across the shaft, leaving you with the bottom of the screw in the hole. In this case there is nothing left to do but to drill out the center of the screw and pick out the rest with dentist's picks.

Having fought out the rust from an old gun, I will now tell you how to put it back. Yes, you may need to know this secret too. It is one that professional gun restorers are least apt to tell you. If you have a flintlock gun with a broken or missing cock or frizzen and have replaced them with brand-new shiny parts, how do you make the new metal blend in with the pitted, dark lock plate and barrel of a New England fowler or a Brown Bess? Simple! Toss the new part or parts into a sauce pan, and several heaping tablespoonsful of Chlorox, cover the parts with water and bring to a boil. Watch the pot as it boils. You will see rust form under your very eyes. Pretty soon, pits and craters will appear, and if you don't watch out the piece will soon be too badly rusted to use. The trick is to watch the rusting process and cut it out just as you approach the condition of the metal you are trying to match. In order to arrest the process, immediately put the metal under running water until it is thoroughly freed from the Chlorox. Also neutralize the surface by putting the piece in a solution of baking soda and water, then wash again. Do not be surprised if the action is not quite arrested and bits of rust continue to form. Keep cleaning the metal, remove the red rust with steel wool, and keep the part well oiled. Eventually the rusting will abate, and you will have a well-antiqued surface.

This is the fast process. In the old days restorers used to bury new parts in a manure pile or just leave them outdoors on the ground for six months to rust. This works very well if you have the time and remember where you buried the part.

Coloring of new stock repairs is tricky. First, try to find old, well-cured wood with which to make the patch or piece. Obviously you want to use the same kind of wood—walnut, mahogony, birch or fruit wood. If you can, try to find an old table or chair leg that has some natural color from aging. I keep a miniature lumber yard of old scraps of wood under my work bench. After picking the best match for your repair, try to match the grain as well, and always be sure that the patch grain runs in the same direction as the stock being worked on. When the patch has been fitted as skillfully as you can, so that there are no gaps to fill and the surface is smooth and continuous with the rest of the stock, you may well need further aging to match the surface oxidation of the rest of the stock. This may range from a charcoal black, found on the most ancient stocks, to the rosy color that walnut gets after it has been around for more than a century.

An ancient, ancient blackened surface can be created by a quick oxidation process with the use of chromium trioxide. This can be obtained in flake form in small quantities in glass jars from a chemical supply house. The flakes are yellow and highly hydroscopic. Dissolve a small quantity in water and apply to the wood with a paint brush you don't care about. The wood will start to turn black in short order. The blacker you want the wood, the more chromium trioxide you paint on. Keep this off your hands and out of your eyes. It is so strong it will begin to dissolve your paint brush.

The beautiful rose color of well-aged walnut or the rippling shades of orange and brown of the tiger maple stocks of Kentucky

The author shoots a hand cannon from Obervillach in Austria. The gun barrel was found in the ground with a load of gunpowder still in the barrel. The stock is a reconstruction after the drawings of da Vinci and Georg Kolderer. The gun had stopped being a shooting gun around 1500.

rifles can be matched by the use of another powerful chemical, nitric acid. Nitric acid can be painted on wood directly, but, again, remember that you are dealing with very powerful stuff which will eat metal, dissolve rubber and plastic bottle caps. It can only be stored in glass, and even there it loses its strength. For safety's sake, buy only a little (which will go a long way in restoration work) and throw away what you don't use. If you live in an apartment, don't pour it down the drain, it might eat out the pipes unless adequately diluted by flushing. A few drops left in the trap won't help matters, so take it out to the curb and pour it in a sewer on a rainy day.

Further finishing of woods and bone inlays can be accomplished with the use of the dyes used to color hand-crafted leathers. These powerful dyes are available in a range of colors at the store which supplies the craft. The stores near me are called Tandy and are part of a chain.

If you get involved in the restoration of very old arms which have ivory, bone or mother-of-pearl inlays, you may find yourself looking for a supply of these materials. Bone is easy. Ask your butcher to save and saw up the femur of the next steer he cuts up. Usually this bone is used for soup or as dog bones for big dogs. If the butcher is your pal, he will run the bone through his saw a few times to give you some flat pieces. This beats sawing it up yourself, though that is not as hard as it looks. Boil the bone in heavily salted water and remove any scraps of tissue and marrow. Then let the bone dry out slowly in a warm place. Do not try to dry the bone in a hot oven unless you want brown bone for inlay. Ivory bits can come from old pieces of broken jewelry, whale bone, etc. If you can't find ivory, you can often substitute bone or horn. In my junk pile I have sawed up pieces of the horns of a moose that a friend of mine shot some years ago. I get mother-of-pearl from the people who supply sea pearl blanks for real pearl shirt buttons.

As a final word of caution, never over restore a gun. You can always do more work on a piece but you cannot undo what you have irrevocably spoiled or destroyed. Don't be a Diderrich; there just aren't enough fine guns around to chance spoiling a single one.

If you think that the cleaning of guns is a new invention of mine, I will leave you with a recipe from the eighteenth century. This is quoted from a book titled *The Discipline of the Light Horse*, by Capt. Hinde, London, 1778.

558 THE DISCIPLINE OF

A Receipt to keep Arms from Ruſt.

One Ounce of Camphire to Two Pounds of Hogs-Lard, Diſſolve them together and take off the Scum; Mix as much Black-Lead as will bring them to an Iron Colour: Rub your Arms over with this, and let it lie on Twenty-four Hours, then Clean them as well as poſſible with a Linen Cloth, and they will keep without the leaſt Ruſt for Six Months.

This recipe comes from an eighteenth-century military manual.

Bibliography

ARMS MAGAZINES

The American Rifleman, Washington, D.C.
Arms Gazette, Los Angeles, California.
The Canadian Journal of Arms Collecting, Ottowa, Ontario, Canada.
Guns and Ammo, Los Angeles, California.
Guns and Hunting, New York, New York.
The Gun Digest, Chicago, Illinois.
Guns Magazine, Skokie, Illinois.
The Gun Report, Aledo, Illinois.
Gun World, Capistrano Beach, California.
Journal of the Arms and Armour Society, London, England.
Zeitschrift für Historische Waffen- und Kostumkunde, Munich, Germany.

ARMS BOOKS

Abridgement of the Patent Specifications Relating to Fire Arms, etc. 1558-1858, Holland Press, London, 1960.

Albaugh, William A. III and Simmons, Edward N. *Confederate Arms*, Stackpole, Harrisburg, Pa., 1957.

Amber, John T. *The Gun Digest* (annual), Chicago, 1944 to date.

————. *The Gun Digest Treasury II* (The best from the first fifteen years of *The Gun Digest*), Chicago, 1956.

————. "This Gun Collecting Game." *The Gun Digest Treasury*, pp. 252–264, Chicago, 1961.

————. *Gun Digest Treasury III*, Chicago, 1966.

Anonymous. *A Short Account of the Worshipful Company of Gunmakers*, London, 1937.

Baxter, D. R. *Superimposed Load Firearms: 1360-1860*, Baxter, Hong Kong, 1966.

————. "Early Lever-Action Repeating Rifles." *Guns Review*, Vol. V, No. 1, London, January, 1965.

————. "English All Metal Flintlock Pistols of the Eighteenth and Early Nineteenth Century." *Armi Antiche*, Turin, 1966.

Bedford, Clay P. *Early Firearms of Great Britain and Ireland from the Collection of Clay P. Bedford*, Metropolitan Museum, New York, 1971.

Belous, Russell E. *A Distinguished Collection of Arms and Armor on Permanent Display at The Los Angeles County Museum of Natural History*, Los Angeles, 1968.

Biringuccio, Vanuccio. *De la Pirotechnia, libri X*, English edition translated by C. S. Smith and Martha T. Gnudi, American Institute of Mining and Metallurgical Engineers, New York, 1943.

Blackmore, Howard L. *British Military Firearms*, Herbert Jenkins, London, 1961.

————. *Guns and Rifles of the World*, Clowes, London and Viking, New York 1965.

Blair, Claude. *European and American Arms*, Batsford, London and Crown, New York, 1962.

————. *Pistols of the World*, Batsford, London, 1968.

Boeheim, Wendelin. *Kunsthistorische Sammlungen des Allerhoöchsten Kaiserhauses, ALBUM hervorragender Gegenstände aus der Waffensammlung*, 2 volumes, Vienna, 1898.

————. *Handbuch der Waffenkunde*, Seemann, Leipzig, 1890.

Boothroyd, Geoffrey. *Gun Collecting*, Arco Publications, London, 1961.

Boston, Noel. *Old Guns and Pistols*, Ernest Benn, London, 1958.

Boudriot, Jean. *Armes aFeu Francaises Modeles Reglementaries*, General Issue French Guns: 1700–1800, Boudriot, Paris, 1963.

Brown, Rodney Hilton. *American Polearms 1526–1865*, N. Flayderman, New Milford, Conn., 1967.

Bulletin des Arquebusiers de France (publication) Les Arquebusiers de France, Paris.

Canby, Courtlandt. *A History of Weaponry* (also published in French and German) Hawthorne, New York, 1963.

Carey, A. Mervin. *English, Irish and Scottish Firearms Makers*, New York, 1954.

Carpegna, Nolfo Di. *Firearms in The Princes Odescalchi Collection in Rome*, Edizioni Marte, Rome, 1968.

Chapel, Charles Edward. *The Gun Collector's Handbook of Values*, Coward-McCann, New York, 1940 and following.

_____. *Guns of the Old West* (500 Illustrations), New York, 1961.

Churchill, Robert. *Churchill's Shotgun Book*, Alfred Knopf, New York, 1955.

Clephan, Robert Coltman. *Firearms from the Earliest Period to About the End of the Fifteenth Century*, Walter Scott, London, 1906 (Facsimile edition, Standard Pubs., Huntington, West Virginia, n.d.).

Cockle, Maurice, J.D. *A Bibliography of Military Books up to 1642*, Holland Press, London, 1957.

Darling, Anthony D. *Red Coat and Brown Bess*, Museum Restoration Service, Toronto, 1971.

Dean, Bashford. *Catalogue of European Court Swords and Hunting Swords*, Metropolitan Museum of Art, New York, 1929.

_____. *The Collection of Arms and Armor of Rutherford*, Stuyvesant, New York, 1914.

De Gheyn, Jacob. *The Exercise of Armes for Calivres, Muskettes, and Pikes after the Order of His Excellence Maurits Prince of Orange . . . Sett Forthe in Figures by Jacob de Gheyn. With Written Instructions for the Service of all Captaines and Comaundours. For to Shewe Hereout the Better Unto Their Yong or Untrayned Soldier the Playne and Perfett Maner to Handle These Armes. They are toe Bye at Amsterdam bye Robert de Boudous*, Amsterdam, 1907, Robert de Boudous, Amsterdam 1607, Reprint, McGraw Hill, New York (c. 1972).

Demmin, August. *Arms and Armour*, George Bell, London, 1877.

Dexter, F. Theodore. *Twenty-Five Year Scrapbook*, Topeka, c. 1937.

_____. *Thirty-Five Years Scrapbook of Antique Arms*. 2 vols., Topeka, Kansas, 1947.

_____. *Forty-Two Years Scrapbook of Rare Ancient Firearms*, Warren F. Lewis, Los Angeles, 1954.

_____. *Half Century Scrapbook of Vari-Type Firearms*, Weaver, Santa Monica, Calif., 1960.

D'Orval, P. *Essay sur les Feux d'artifice pour le Spectacle et pour la Guerre* (Ill.), Paris, 1745.

Dowell, W. C. *The Webley Story* (Ill.), 1962.

Dunlap, Jack. *American, British and Continental Pepperbox Firearms*, Dunlap, Los Altos, Calif., 1964.

Edwards, William B. *Civil War Guns*, Stackpole, Harrisburg, Pa., 1962.

Engelhardt, Baron Armin and Alexander Constantin. "The Story of European Proof Marks." *The Gun Digest*, Chicago, 1952-1961.

Essenwein, A. *Quellen zur Geschichte der Feuerwaffen* (Encyclopedic history of firearms with pictures), Leipzig, 1877, Repr. by Akademische Druck-Verlagsanstalt, Graz, 1967.

ffoulkes, C. J. *European Arms and Armour in the University of Oxford*, Oxford, 1912.

_____. *Inventory and Survey of the Armories of the Tower of London*, Proof Marks, 2 vols., London, 1915.

————. *Some account of the Worshipful Company of Armourers and Braziers—Together with a Catalogue,* Privately printed, 1927.

Frith, James. *Antique Pistol Collecting (1400-1860) (illustrated),* Gunmakers Marks, 1960.

Frost, H. Gordon. *Blades and Barrels,* Walloon Press, El Paso, Texas, 1972.

————. *Six Centuries of Combination Weapons,* Walloon Press, El Paso, Texas, 1972.

Fuller, Claude C. *The Whitney Firearms,* Standard, Huntington, W. Va., 1946.

Gaibi, General Agostino. *Le Armi da Fuoco Portatili Italiane,* Bramante Editrice, s.p.a., Milan, 1962.

Gardner, Colonel Robert E. *Small Arms Makers, A Directory of Fabricators of Firearms, etc.,* Crown, New York, 1963.

George, J. N. *English Guns and Rifles,* Stackpole, Harrisburg, Pa., 1947.

————. *English Pistols and Revolvers,* Samworth, Harrisburg, Pa., 1947.

Gerrare, Wirt (William Oliver Greener). *A Bibliography of Guns and Shooting,* Roxburghe Press, London, 1895.

Gilchrist, Helen Ives. *A Catalogue of the Collections of Arms and Armour Presented to the Cleveland Museum of Art by Mr. and Mrs. John Long Severance,* Cleveland, 1924.

Gluckman, Arcadi and Satterlee, L. D. *American Gun Makers,* Ulbrich, Buffalo, N. Y., 1945.

Gluckman, Arcadi. *Identifying Old U.S. Muskets, Rifles and Carbines,* Stackpole, Harrisburg, Pa., 1959–1960.

————. *United States Martial Pistols and Revolvers,* Stackpole, Harrisburg, Pa., 1939, 1960.

Grancsay, Stephen V. *The Bashford Dean Collection of Arms and Armour in the Metropolitan Museum of Art,* Southworth, Portland, Maine, 1933.

————. *Early Firearms of Great Britain and Ireland from the Collection of Clay P. Bedford,* Metropolitan Museum of Art, New York, 1971.

————. *Master French Gunsmiths' Designs XVII-XIX Centuries Jacquinet, Thuraine, LeHollandois, Picquot, Marcou, Berain, Daubigny, Simonin, de la Feuille, Weigel, Sandrart, Raab, Fiscione, Rennesson, Claesen,* Winchester Press, New York, 1970.

Grancsay, Stephen V. and Lindsay, Merrill. *Illustrated British Firearms Patents,* Winchester Press, New York, 1947.

Grant, James J. *Single-Shot Rifles,* William Morrow, New York, 1947.

————. *More Single-Shot Rifles,* William Morrow, New York, 1959.

Greener, W. W. *The Gun and Its Development,* Longman, Rees, Orme, Brown, Green and Longman, London, 1835 (and numerous succeeding editions) including Bonanza, Crown, N.Y., n.d.

Grose, Francis. *Military Antiquities Respecting a History of the English Army and a Treatise on Ancient Armour,* S. Hooper, London 1786–1789, plus 1801, 1812, repr. of 1786 ed. Benchmark, Glendale, N.Y., 1970.

Gun Digest Treasury (The best from the first 15 years of the Gun Digest), Chicago, 1956.

Halsey, Ashley, Jr. N.R.A. Gun Collectors Guide, N.R.A., Washington, D.C., 1973.

Hanson, Charles E., Jr. The Plains Rifle, Bramhall, New York, 1960.

Harris, Clive. A History of the Birmingham Gun-Barrel Proof House, Birmingham, 1946.

Hatch, A. Remington Arms in American History, Reinhart & Co., New York, 1956.

Haven, C.T. and Belden, F.A. A History of the Colt Revolver, William Morrow, New York, 1940.

Hayward, John F. The Art of the Gunmaker, Volumes I and II, Barrie & Rockliff, London, 1962 and 1963, 2nd revised edition, 1965.

_____. European Firearms, H.M. Stationery Office, London, 1958.

Held, Robert. The Age of Firearms/A Pictorial History, Harper, New York, 1957.

_____. Arms and Armor Annual, Digest Books, Northfield, Illinois, 1973.

Henderson, James. Firearms Collecting for Amateurs, Frederick Muller, London, 1966.

Hewitt, John. Ancient Armour and Weapons in Europe (3 vols.), John Henry & James Parker, Oxford, 1855-1860. Reprinted by Akademische Druck - und Verlagsanstalt, Graz, Austria, 1967.

_____. "Notice of the Combined Use of the Match-lock and the Flintlock." Archaeological Journal, 1860.

Hoff, Dr. Arne. Feuerwaffen I and II (877 pages), Klinkhardt & Bierman Braunschweig, Germany, 1969.

Hoopes, Thomas T. "The Function of the Perfected Lorenzoni Repeating Flintlock System." Arms and Armor Annual, pp. 216, 226, 1973.

_____. "Notes on the Development of the Baltic Flintlock" A Miscellany of Arms and Armor, pp. 45-51, Rudge, New York, 1927.

_____. "The Double Set Trigger." A Miscellany of Arms and Armor, pp. 36-38, Rudge, New York, 1927.

_____. "A Decimal Classification of the Discharge Mechanism of Hand Firearms" (with William G. Renwick). A Miscellany of Arms and Armor, pp. 64-103, Rudge, New York, 1927.

_____. Armor and Arms, St. Louis City Art Museum, 1954.

_____. "Two Early Revolvers." The American Rifleman, Vol. XCV, No. 2, February, 1947.

Johnson, Melvin M. Jr., and Haven, Charles T. Automatic Arms, Their History, Development and Use, Morrow, New York, 1941.

Johnson, Peter H. Parker/America's Finest Shotgun, Stackpole/Bonanza, 1961.

Karr, Charles & Carroll. Remington Handguns, Military Publishing Co., U.S.A., 1947.

Kauffman, Henry J. *Early American Gunsmiths: 1650 - 1850*, Bramhall House, New York, 1952.

————. *The Pennsylvania-Kentucky Rifle*, Harrisburg, 1960.

Keith, Neal, W. and Back, D.H. *Forsyth & Co.: Patent Gunmakers*, G. Bell & Sons, London, 1969.

————. *The Mantons: Gunmakers*, Walker & Co., New York, 1967, Herbert Jenkens, London.

Keith, Neal, W. *Collecting Duelling Pistols*, Arms and Armour Press, London, 1968.

————. *Spanish Guns and Pistols*, Benn, London, 1955.

Kentucky Rifle Association. *The Kentucky Rifle, A True American Heritage in Pictures*, K.R.A., Washington, D.C., 1968.

Kienbusch, C.O. von. *Kretzschmar von Kienbusch Collection of Armor and Arms*, Princeton University, Princeton, 1963.

Kienbusch, C.O. von and Grancsay, Stephen V. *The Bashford Dean Collection of Arms and Armour in the Metropolitan Museum of Art*, Portland, Maine, 1933.

Kindig, Joe, Jr. *Thoughts on the Kentucky Rifle in Its Golden Age*, Hyatt, Wilmington, Del., 1960 and Shumway, York, Pa., 1971.

Kuhlhoff, Peter and Koller, Larry. *Guns – The Complete Book – All Guns – All Ammunition*, Maco, 1953.

Kulhoff, Peter; Hall, Thomas; and Watrous, George. *The History of Winchester Firearms: 1866 - 1966*, North Haven, 1966.

Laking, Sir Guy Francis. *Wallace Collection at the Hertford House*, Revised by Sir James G. Mann, Darling & Son, London, 1900.

————. *A Record of European Armour and Arms Through Seven Centuries (1000 - 1700)* (5 vols.), G. Bell & Sons, London, 1920–1922.

Lavin, James D. *A History of Spanish Firearms*, Arco, New York, 1965.

Lindsay, Merrill K. and Grancsay, Stephen. *Master French Gunsmith's Designs*, Winchester Press, New York, 1970.

————. *Miniature Arms*, McGraw Hill and Winchester Press, New York, 1970.

————. *One Hundred Great Guns*, Walker, New York, 1967.

————. *Illustrated British Firearms Patents*, Winchester Press, New York, 1970.

————. Numerous articles in *American Heritage, Argosy, Armi Antiche, Guns Magazine, The Gun Report, Time Magazine, True*, etc.

Lindsay, Merrill K. and Grancsay, Stephen. *Master French Gunsmith's Designs*, Winchester Press, New York, 1970.

Logan, Herschel C. *Cartridges*, Standard, Huntington, W. Va., 1948.

London. *A Short Account of the Worshipful Company of Gunmakers* (Anon.), London, 1937.

McHenry and Roper, Walter F. *Smith & Wesson Hand Guns*, Standard Publications, Huntington, W. Va., 1945.

Madis, George. *The Winchester Book*, Madis, Dallas, 1961.

Mann, F.W. *The Bullets' Flight (1909)*, Ray Riling, Philadelphia, 1965.

Mann, Sir James G. *Wallace Collection Catalogues—European Arms and Armour* (2 vols., including bibliography), Clowes, London, 1962.

Moore, Warren. *Guns, the Development of Firearms, Airguns and Cartridges*, Grosset & Dunlap, New York, 1967.

————. *Weapons of the American Revolution and Accountrements*, Funk & Wagnalls, New York, 1967.

Muller, John. *A Treatise of Artillery* (3rd ed.), John Millan, London, 1780, Reprinted with a preface by H.L. Peterson by Museum Restoration Service, Ottawa, Ontario, Canada, 1965.

Munhall, Burton D. *See* White, Henry P.

Louis Napoleon on Artillery XIV to XVII Century, Illustrations with text by W.Y. Carman, National Army Museum, Arms & Armour Press, London, 1967.

Neal, Robert J. and Jinks, Roy J. *Smith and Wesson: 1857 - 1945*, A.S. Barnes, New York, 1966.

Neumann, George C. *The History of Weapons of the American Revolution*, Harper & Row, New York, 1967.

Nickel, Helmut. *Warriors and Worthies*, Atheneum, New York, 1969.

————. "The Armorers Shop." *Bulletin of the Metropolitan Museum of Art*, Dec. 1969.

————. "The Little Knights of the Living Room Table." *Bulletin of the Metropolitan Museum of Art*, Dec. 1966.

North, Simeon N.D. and Ralph H. *Simeon North, First Official Pistol Maker of the United States*, Rumford Press, Concord, N.H., 1913.

Nutter, Waldo E. *Manhattan Firearms*, Stackpole Co., Harrisburg, Pa., 1958.

Parsons, John E. *The First Winchester, The Story of the 1866 Repeating Rifle*, Morrow, N.Y., 1955, Winchester Press, N.Y. 1969.

————. *The Peacemaker and Its Rivals*, Morrow, N.Y., 1950.

————. *Smith & Wesson Revolvers*, Morrow, N.Y., 1957.

Peterson, Harold L. *Arms and Armor in Colonial America, 1526 - 1783*, Bramhall House, New York, 1956.

————. *Encyclopedia of Firearms*, Dutton, New York, 1964.

————. "Famous Firearms." Series of short illustrated articles which ran in *The American Rifleman*, Washington, D.C. and reprinted in the *N.H.A. Gun Collectors Guide.*

————. *The Treasury of the Gun*, Golden Press, 1962.

————. *The Pageant of the Gun*, Doubleday, New York, 1967.

————. *The Remington Historical Treasury of American Guns*, Thomas Nelson, New York, 1966, Plus numerous articles in: *American Rifleman, Gun Collector, Guns and Hunting* and *Muzzle Blasts*.

Reid, Sir Alexander John Forsyth. *Alexander John Forsyth*, University Press, Aberdeen, Scotland, 1909.

Ricketts, Howard. *Firearms*, Weidenfeld, London, 1962.

Riling, Ray. *Guns and Shooting, a Bibliography*, Riling, Greenberg, New York, 1951.

Roberts, Ned H. *The Muzzle-Loading Cap Lock Rifle*, Bonanza, N.Y. 1940 - 1952.

Roper. *See* McHenry.

Russell, Carl P. *Guns on the Early Frontiers*, Bonanza, New York, 1957.

Satterlee, L.D. and Gluckman, Arcadi. *American Gun Makers*, Ulbrich, Buffalo, 1945.

Schedelmann, Hans. *Die Grossen Büchsenmacher*, Klinkhardt & Biermann, Braunschweig, Germany, 1972.

Serven, James E. *The Collecting of Guns*, Stackpole, Harrisburg, 1964.

————. *Colt Firearms 1836 - 1958*, Santa Ana, California, 1964.

Shumway, George. *Long Rifles of Note, Pennsylvania*, Shumway, York, Pa., 1968.

Smith, Captain George. *An Universal Military Dictionary*, Printed for J. Millan, London, 1779, Reprinted Museum Restoration Service, Ottawa, Canada, 1969.

Smith, Samuel E. *American Percussion Revolvers*, Museum Restoration Service, Ottowa, Canada, 1971.

Smith, W.H.B. *Pistols and Revolvers*, Military Service Publishing Co., Harrisburg, Pa., 1946.

Smith, W.H. B. and Joseph E. *Small Arms of the World*, Stackpole, Harrisburg, Pa., 1949, 1962.

————. *The Book of Rifles* (3rd ed.), Stackpole, Harrisburg, Pa., 1963.

Smith, Winston O. *The Sharps Rifle*, Morrow, New York, 1943.

Stockbridge, V.D. *Digest of Patents Relating to Breech-Loading and Magazine Small Arms (1863 - 1873)*, Washington, 1874, reprint by Norman Flayderman, 1963.

Stone, George Cameron. *Glossary of the Construction, Decoration and Use of Arms and Armor*, Southport, Portland, Maine, 1934, reprint New York, 1961.

Swayze, Nathan L. *'51 Colt Navies*, Taylor Publishing Co., Dallas, Texas, 1967.

Tarassuk, Leonid. "The Collection of Arms and Armour in the State Hermitage, Leningrad," Part II: "The Collection of Russian Arms and Armour," *J.A.A.S.*, Vol. V, Nos. 4 - 5, pp. 205 - 216, London, March, 1966.

————. *Russian Pistols in the Seventeenth Century*, Arms and Armour Press, London, 1968.

————. *Antique European and American Firearms at the Hermitage Museum*, Arma Press, North Branford, Connecticut, 1971.

Thomas, Bruno; Gamber, Ortwin; and Schedelmann, Hans. *Arms and Armour of the Western World*, McGraw Hill, New York, 1964.

Tout, T.F. "Firearms in England in the 14th Century," *English Historical Review*, XXVI, No. 104, pp. 66, 702, (669 - 668), October 1911, reprint with an Introduction by Claude Blair, Arms and Armour Press, Lionel Leventhal Limited, London, 1968.

Valencia, Don Juan de El Conde Vdo. *Catalogo de las Armas del Instituto de Valencia de Don Juan*, Florit & Arescun and Sanchez Canton, Madrid, 1927.

————. *Spanish Arms and Armour*, translated by Albert F. Calvert, John Lane, N.Y. and London, n.d., (The Ameria Real Collection)

Van Rensselaer, Stephen. *American Firearms*, New York, 1947.

Wahl, Paul and Toppel, Don. *The Gatling Gun*, Herbert Jenkins, London, 1966.

Watrous, George. *Winchester Rifles and Shotguns* (2nd ed.), New Haven, Conn., 1950.

Whelan, Major Townsend. *The American Rifle*, The Century Co., New York, 1918.

White, Henry P. and Munhall, Burton D. *Pistol and Revolver Cartridges*, A.S. Barnes, Cranbury, N.J., 1948 - 1967.

Whitelaw, C.E. and Jackson. *A Treatise on Scottish Hand Firearms*, Holland Press, London, 1959.

Wilkinson, Frederick. *Arms and Armour*, A. & C. Black, London, 1963.

————. *Small Arms*, Hawthorne Books, New York, 1966.

Williamson, Harold F. *Winchester, the Gun That Won the West*, Combat Forces Press, Washington, D.C., 1952.

Wilson, R.L. *The Arms Collection of Colonel Colt*, Herb Glass, Bullville, N.Y., 1964.

————. *The Book of Colt Firearms* (Sutherland Collection) (420 color plates, 1258 B & W), Kansas City, 1972.

————. *Colt Commemorative Firearms*, Hartford, 1969.

Winant, Lewis. *Early Percussion Firearms*, London, 1961.

————. *Firearms Curiosa*, St. Martin's Press, New York, 1955.

————. *Pepperbox Firearms*, New York, 1952.

Wolff, Eldon B. *Air Guns*, Milwaukee Public Museum, Milwaukee, 1958.

Index